LOBBY FOR YOUR LIBRARY

KNOW WHAT WORKS

Lisa F. Kinney

American Library Association 1992
Chicago and London

Cover design by Charles Bozett
Text design by Dianne Rooney

Composed by Digital Graphics, Inc. in Palatino using T_EX.
Reproduction copy set on a Varityper 4300P phototypesetter

Printed on 50-pound Finch Opaque, a pH-neutral stock, and bound in
10 point C1S cover stock by IPC, St. Joseph, Michigan

The paper used in this publication meets the minimum requirements of
American National Standard for Information Sciences—Permanence of
Paper for Printed Library Materials, ANSI Z39.48–1984. ∞

Library of Congress Cataloging-in-Publication Data

Kinney, Lisa.
    Lobby for your library : knowing what works / Lisa F. Kinney.
      p.   cm.
    Includes index.
    ISBN 0-8389-3410-2 (alk. paper)
    1. Library fund raising—Political aspects—United States.
2. Libraries and state—United States. 3. Lobbying—United States.
I. Title.
    Z683.2.U6K56   1992
    021.8'3'0973—dc20
                                                92-9142
                                               CIP

Printed in the United States of America.

96 95 94 93 92   5 4 3 2 1

Contents

List of Tables

Acknowledgments

I would like to thank Eloise Kinney for her encouragement and moral support; Bill Schmich for his ongoing creativity and imagination; Wyoming State Senators John Vinich, Bob Reese, and Liz Byrd for using their names and gracious personalities; Ruth Poe for the perpetual fun her name gives our family; Herbert Bloom for his patience and debate; Judy Zelenski for her persistence in keeping me involved with libraries; and Dr. Phyllis Kinney for always helping when needed. Very special thanks to my patient husband Rodney P. Lang for giving me time to work on this book, and to my wonderful children Cambria, Shelby, and Eli for providing me with continual humorous interludes and a source of joy and inspiration.

Introduction

Why is there a need for a book on lobbying for libraries? Libraries and librarians are survivors. In today's world of technology, hard economic times, and never-ending competition with other public services, television, and videos, library use is nevertheless increasing. The demand for instantaneous information, books, and other media is also increasing. For the most part, libraries continue to provide these services free of charge. Libraries are still "people's universities." Weaker species have died out, but libraries have evolved to meet today's demands while maintaining yesterday's recognition of the value of libraries and the power of information.

In order to continue to survive, librarians must play an increasingly political role as the twenty-first century approaches. Librarians need to become politically active if they are not already and politically astute if they hope to remain competitive.

This book attempts to serve as a primer for the self-avowed apolitical librarian who has come to realize the importance of being politically earnest. Within this book librarians will find reasons for and ways and means of lobbying. Although many lobbying techniques can be used in every library situation, the book devotes several chapters to different types of libraries and attempts to tailor examples to each library's lobbying needs. Additionally, one chapter provides universal lobbying techniques librarians can use regardless of library type.

This book does not specifically discuss the lobbying needs of special libraries, because so many are nongovernmental. However, special libraries certainly face the same kind of internal politics when procuring a budget that other libraries do. Consequently, special librarians are urged to look at the chapters dealing with school and academic libraries where much of the battle is internal before it reaches any decision-making bodies. In addition, special librarians will find techniques scattered throughout the book that they can adapt to their own situations.

A second area not covered in this book is running for a political office. As a librarian, I turned to politics when I could not make any progress "on the outside." Running for office is a very effective method to increase library awareness in a political district. Even if you are not elected, a political campaign provides a librarian with a tremendous opportunity to speak out on behalf of libraries. Some limits and dangers exist. Obviously, a county librarian cannot hold a political position at the county level but can run for a statewide office. A danger is revealing your preferred political party, which may bother some of your patrons or your funding decision makers. On the other hand, if your mission is to help libraries, running for office is a laudable goal and most people will not hold your partisan affiliation against you.

The "p-word" (*politics*) is a dirty word to many, but politics can be fun and fruitful if approached in a positive and practical way. With luck, this book will not only assist librarians in lobbying techniques but will also support and encourage those librarians ready to throw their hats (books?) into the ring of the political world.

Overview of Federal Influence and Issues

Library-Funding Legislation

Federal library funds provide only 4 percent of the total dollars libraries spend.[1] Although federal funds comprise only a small part of their overall budget, libraries rely on these funds, which stimulate library development and services at the state and local levels. That these funds exist is a tribute to the library world which initially persuaded the federal government that local public libraries need federal aid.[2]

An aspect of federal funding that is sometimes confusing to the "receiving end" is the difference between authorizing and appropriating funding. Congress authorizes a program by creating a statute that outlines what a particular program can do and who or what will benefit from it. Programs are authorized for a certain number of years, and then they must be reauthorized. Without funding, the program simply exists on paper. Congress must appropriate dollars to implement the concept it authorized. Even though the original enactment may authorize specific dollar amounts for a certain program, Congress must actually appropriate tax dollars for the same program before any money is available to filter down to the local level. Congress may choose to appropriate funds in one budgetary cycle but not in the next.

As the national debt increases, Congress and the president continually try to find new ways to reduce this ever-increasing liability. A traditional method is to try to transfer responsibility for funding certain programs to the states instead of continuing federal sponsorship. Federal library-funding programs have not yet succumbed to this fate, although federal library funding remains an ongoing struggle. For example, in 1991, the president's proposed budget for libraries contained no funding for Title II of the Higher Education Act or for the Library Services and Construction Act (LSCA), with the exception of $35 million for literacy programs. Although the Washington office of the American Library Association and state librarians shoulder a majority of the lobbying efforts for federal funds, librarians must be cognizant of the federal funding scene and help when possible.

Ongoing funding for the programs discussed below is a direct result of the lobbying effort of the American Library Association and librarians throughout the United States. The continuing successful appropriations for federal library programs serve as an excellent example of what a good lobbying effort can accomplish on behalf of libraries.

Library Services Act and Library Services and Construction Act

The major piece of federal legislation affecting public libraries is the Library Services and Construction Act, formerly the Library Services Act (LSA). Title III of the act also provides funding for academic and school libraries under some conditions. The act is a categorical grant program that is allocated by formula and distributed to the states. In turn, the states distribute the funds to local libraries.

When first signed into law in 1956, the LSA contained only one title, "Public Library Services," and provided funds only to towns with fewer than 10,000 inhabitants.[3] The state library was designated as distributor of the funds. The rural nature of the program changed in 1964 when the original act was replaced by the LSCA and title II, Public Library Construction, was added. Since making the major changes in 1964, Congress has frequently amended the LSCA.[4] In 1966, amendments added Title III, Interlibrary Cooperation, and Title IV, Specialized State Library Services, which included Part A, State Institutional Library Services, and Part B, Library Services to the Physically Handicapped. In 1970, Title IV was consolidated with Title I. Not many changes were made to the LSCA until 1984 when three additional titles were created: IV: Library Services for Indian Tribes, V: Foreign Language Materials Acquisition, and VI: Library Literacy Programs. In 1990, two new titles were passed: Title VII, Evaluation and Assessment, and Title VIII, Library Learning Center Programs, including Part A, Family Learning Centers, and Part B, Library Literacy Centers. Neither new title has yet been funded.[5] The evolving needs of libraries and the concomitant lobbying efforts required to amend the LSCA are reflected in these changes to the legislation.

A brief overview of each title demonstrates the library community's efforts in the federal lobbying arena. Title I was authorized to provide formula grants to the states to assist public libraries in establishing, expanding, and improving library services. Among other things, these funds may be used to provide library access for the handicapped, community information referral services, literacy and drug abuse programs, and library services to day-care centers. They may also be used to support and expand the services of major urban resource libraries and to strengthen metropolitan libraries serving as regional resource centers.[6]

Title II provides formula grants to the states to assist public libraries in new construction, or acquisition, remodeling, and alteration of existing buildings. Some types of equipment also may be purchased with Title II funds.[7]

Title III affects not only public libraries but also school and academic libraries. The purpose of this title is to provide formula grants to states to develop, establish, expand, or operate local, state, regional, and interstate cooperative library networks and to promote resource sharing among all kinds of libraries.[8]

The second Title IV, created after the original Title IV was consolidated with Title I, deals with library services for Indian tribes and Hawaiian natives. The purpose of this title is to develop and improve public library services to these two groups on a noncompetitive, equal-allotment-per-eligible-tribe basis. The funds may be used to assess tribal library needs, for personnel salaries and training, for purchase of library materials, for construction, renovation, or remodeling of library buildings, and more.[9]

Title V provides grants to state and local public libraries to purchase foreign language materials. Although this title was established in 1984, Congress appropriated funds for it for the first time in 1991.[10]

Title VI of the LSCA provides grants to state and local public libraries to support literacy programs. State libraries may use funding to coordinate and plan library literacy programs and to train librarians and volunteers to implement literacy programs. Public libraries may use funding to promote volunteer services by individuals, agencies, and organizations involved in literacy programs and to acquire library materials for literacy programs.[11]

Title VII of the LSCA, Evaluation and Assessment, authorizes $500,000 for the Secretary of Education to establish a program to evaluate and assess LSCA programs. As mentioned previously, this title has yet to be funded.[12]

Finally, Title VIII, Library Learning Center Programs, consists of two parts. Part A is Family Learning Centers. This section authorizes direct discretionary grants up to $200,000 to public libraries to expand and improve opportunities for lifetime learning and for involving families in the education of their children.[13] If funded, Part B would accomplish three purposes: (1) establish model library literacy centers to disseminate literacy materials and equipment to public libraries; (2) help illiterate adults obtain full employment; and (3) offer innovative approaches to improving library literacy for adults.[14]

Funding for Title VIII cannot be appropriated unless total funding for LSCA Titles I, II, and III "exceeds the previous year's total by at least four percent."[15]

The LSCA is administered by Library Programs, a unit within the Office of Educational Research and Improvement in the United States Department of Education. The agency was created in the 1930s when the push for federal aid to public libraries was first conceived. Although it has operated as a section, a branch, a division, and a bureau in the past, it has consistently stayed within the national education institution and provided a stable overseeing function for library legislation.[16]

Has the LSCA positively affected library services in the United States? The answer is yes, of course. But when Congress asks this question of librarians, can they back up their "yes" answer with documentation and proof? A group of individuals and libraries are attempting to evaluate the effect of the LSCA on public library services in the United States. The Federal-State Cooperative System for Public Library Data (FSCS) was developed to encourage uniform reporting of library statistics gathered by state libraries and to help coordinate this information with the periodic reporting of national public library statistics by the National Center for Education Statistics (NCES).[17]

Once FSCS is in full operational gear, current national library data will be available and updated regularly. When these statistics are compiled, national evaluators can analyze the libraries receiving LSCA funding to determine the actual effect of the program on library services.[18] This evaluation can be presented to Congress as part of a lobbying effort to show that the tax dollars being allocated to libraries are well spent. Legislators like to receive documentation on programs they fund to justify continued funding and to ensure the program is actually working and having the effect intended by the legislation. Just saying a legislatively funded program is good is insufficient to persuade decision makers that further funding of the program is justified. Accountability based on statistics is essential to ongoing legislative support.

The Higher Education Act of 1965, Title II

The major piece of federal legislation affecting academic library funding is the Higher Education Act of 1965, Title II. At the time it was passed, half of the libraries in institutions of higher learning in the United States failed to meet minimum library standards. Fifteen universities with doctoral programs had fewer than 150,000 volumes, and 82 percent of community colleges had inadequate collections.[19] Consequently, the passage of this act was welcomed heartily in the academic library community.

Originally, Title II A of the bill provided for acquisition of library materials. Funding under this section gradually diminished until 1983, at which time Congress discontinued funding altogether.[20] The other legislated sections of Title II (B and C) have fared better, and a new Title II D was added when the Higher Education Act was reauthorized in 1986.

Title II B has two main components: (1) education and training, and (2) research and demonstration. The first part of Title II B authorizes funds to educate and train library and information personnel in library degree programs or nondegree professional programs. The second part of Title II B provides grants for projects to improve libraries, to educate and train for the profession, and to disseminate information derived from these projects.[21] Priorities in funding projects may be established from year to year. For example, during the 1991 fiscal year, priority in the career training portion of the bill was given to train or retrain library personnel in areas of library specialization where there were shortages, such as science-reference librarians and children's and young-adult librarians, and to increase excellence in library education by encouraging study in librarianship at the doctoral level.[22]

Title II C originally provided funding through the Office of Education to the Library of Congress to acquire and catalog scholarly materials worldwide. The Library of Congress later funded this program out of its own appropriations, and in 1976 a new Title II C was created to provide support for major research libraries.[23] Research libraries can use these funds to preserve and strengthen their collections through acquisition of materials and to make their resources accessible to outside researchers and scholars. Applicants must meet the requirements of the definition of a major research library. Authorized activities include everything from acquisition of materials to creating indices and hiring additional staff to carry out a particular project.[24]

The most recent addition to this act is Title II D, which authorizes grants to institutions of higher education to improve library services through advanced technology. Four types of grants are available: (1) networking grants to institutions of higher learning with special needs in the area of resource-sharing; (2) grants to combinations of institutions of higher learning for joint-use library activities; (3) grants to public or private nonprofit organizations which provide library and information services to institutions of higher education on a formal cooperative basis; and (4) research and demonstration grants to institutions of higher learning to support projects to meet special national or regional needs by using new technology.[25]

The authorization for the Higher Education Act of 1965 expired at the end of September 1991. The American Library Association effectively lobbied Congress by passing a resolution asking Congress to reauthorize the act and to change parts of Title II.[26] Members of Congress expect to receive resolutions such as this from special interest organizations concerning legislation that affects the members of their organizations. Resolutions provide valuable information to members of Congress by representing a consensus of a large group of individuals affected either by the proposed legislation or by the *sunsetting* (establishing an ending date for the statute as part of the legislative enactment) associated with a particular piece of legislation, as in this case. When a special interest group does not respond at all to legislation affecting it, the silence speaks as loudly as a resolution. Congress will assume that no one objects to the proposed changes. Therefore, the association's action is laudable and should be followed, when possible, by state associations facing state laws affecting libraries.

Elementary and Secondary Education Act and Education Consolidation and Improvement Act

School libraries and media centers are eligible for federal funds under the Elementary and Secondary Education Act (ESEA), which was signed into law in 1965. Under Title II of this law, federal funds became available for the first time to acquire library materials for public and private elementary and secondary schools.[27] During its first year, Title II stimulated the establishment of 3,250 elementary and secondary public school media centers throughout the United States. Between 1964 and 1974, it increased the number of libraries in schools with 150 or more students from 56,000 to 74,725.[28] ESEA Title II helped the school library become an integral part of the total school instructional program.[29]

Title II existed until 1974, at which time the Education Amendments of 1974 were adopted. School library aid was combined with two other programs into Title IV B of the ESEA, effective in 1976. The legislation changed the program from one of categorical federal funding for school libraries to state-administered block grants.[30] Since that time, Congress has amended the law several times. One of the more important changes was the replacement of the ESEA by the Education Consolidation and Improvement Act (ECIA) in 1981.

ECIA Chapter 2 incorporated ESEA IV B. States received a grant allocation depending on the number of enrolled pupils and were required to distribute 80 percent to local education agencies. These local agencies then had discretion to use the money for a variety of purposes, one of which was to support school media centers. Under ECIA Chapter 2, the level of federal support for school media centers actually decreased substantially because the focus of the legislation switched from specifically funding school media centers to funding school media centers as only one of several potential recipients.[31]

In 1988, Congress reauthorized Chapter 2 for five years (1988–1993) as ESEA Title I, Chapter 2, Federal, State, and Local Partnership for Education Improvement, which contains some general provisions affecting school media centers.[32] Under this new act, school library resources remain one of the six targeted areas of assistance, as compared to the thirty-two categories authorized for funding under ECIA Chapter 2. Elementary and secondary school librarians must be appointed to the required state advisory committees by governors in states participating in the program. The act clarifies that Chapter 1, Aid to Disadvantaged Children, may be used to acquire school library resources and train librarians. Grants under this act may also be used to purchase instructional materials, including library books, textbooks, and audiovisual materials and equipment.[33]

Because this is a fairly new program, it is difficult to determine how much actual support this act will provide for school libraries. However, it appears that, once again, a consolidation of funding legislation may result in an actual dollar decrease for school libraries.[34]

Comprehensive Employment and Training Act and Job Training Partnership Act

In 1973, Congress passed the Comprehensive Employment and Training Act (CETA), which provided job training and employment opportunities for the economically disadvantaged, the unemployed, and the underemployed.[35] Public and school libraries took advantage of this program to fill both professional and staff positions, because libraries were eligible under the federal guidelines. In 1982, Congress replaced CETA with the Job Training Partnership Act (JTPA), and, as a result, school libraries unfortunately were no longer able to fill positions with these funds.

Lobbying at the Federal Level

The Washington Office of the American Library Association

Over the years, the Washington Office of the American Library Association has been extremely effective in nurturing legislation that positively affects libraries, in killing bad legislation, and in keeping the library world abreast of both types of legislation. Whenever librarians are concerned about federal level legislation, a good way to start is to contact this ALA office.[36] It has handouts, informational brochures, names of contact people, and everything else a librarian might need to approach a federal elected official.

Federal Funding of Library Programs

Federal library legislation has been thoroughly discussed. However, because of the ever-changing nature of congressional legislation, a librarian-lobbyist interested in one of the federal funding programs should always check with ALA in Washington or with his or her own representatives before writing a letter about a particular piece of legislation.

White House Conferences

The library world as a whole received excellent national publicity from the two White House Conferences. Although the conferences are controversial within the library community itself, to most outsiders they serve as a reminder of the importance of libraries. A national, concerted effort that focuses on libraries can be an extremely effective tool to highlight libraries and the unique role they play in American society. Even though the impact of the second conference will not be known for a while, the library world should anticipate and plan for a third one.

General Tips

THE ART OF LOBBYING AT THE FEDERAL LEVEL

Most librarians will get only superficially involved with lobbying at the federal level. The ALA Washington Office serves as the national association's lobbyist and does an excellent job. Local librarians can be helpful as part of the constituency bulk but usually will not spearhead a nationwide effort.

PASSAGE OF A BILL THROUGH CONGRESS

Federal legislation follows a path very similar to that of state legislation.

Table 1   How a Bill Becomes Law at the Federal Level

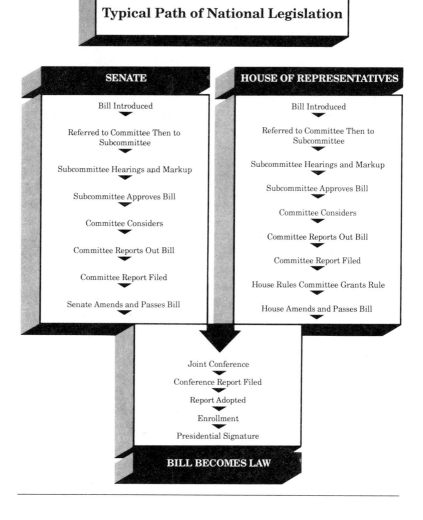

Typical Path of National Legislation

SENATE	HOUSE OF REPRESENTATIVES
Bill Introduced	Bill Introduced
Referred to Committee Then to Subcommittee	Referred to Committee Then to Subcommittee
Subcommittee Hearings and Markup	Subcommittee Hearings and Markup
Subcommittee Approves Bill	Subcommittee Approves Bill
Committee Considers	Committee Considers
Committee Reports Out Bill	Committee Reports Out Bill
Committee Report Filed	Committee Report Filed
Senate Amends and Passes Bill	House Rules Committee Grants Rule
	House Amends and Passes Bill

Joint Conference
Conference Report Filed
Report Adopted
Enrollment
Presidential Signature

BILL BECOMES LAW

RESOURCES

Several good books and articles have been written on libraries and lobbying at the federal level.[37] Individuals interested in federal lobbying efforts for libraries should read some of these books or articles that deal specifically with congressional lobbying techniques.

Many of the general tips in this book will apply when dealing with congressional representatives and senators.

Since the amount of federal funding for libraries is so small compared to that of the state and local share, a librarian should place his or her greatest effort locally and follow the lead of the ALA office for issues of national concern.

Censorship

Libraries need to lobby decision makers at all levels of government for more than just funding. Librarians have traditionally opposed censorship, in spite of potential public criticism against individuals or organizations which work to ensure that laws involving access to materials are not overly broad or ambiguous. The library profession has consistently resisted efforts to restrict access to information. The American Library Association's "Library Bill of Rights" is an example of the strong stance librarians have taken in this area.[38]

Librarians face two outside sources of censorship: the government and special interest groups.[39] Often it is hard to distinguish between the two because special interest groups often pressure government into censoring materials. Although the focus of this chapter is federal issues, all levels of government have attempted to censor information at one time or another, and censorship affects all libraries.

Local Level

At the local level, school boards notoriously censor books in school libraries, often because of one complaint from one parent.[40] Lobby efforts in this area can serve to dissuade such a knee-jerk reaction if school librarians are organized ahead of time and prepared to face such a problem. A written selection policy that specifically deals with censorship and is incorporated into a policy manual will take care of most problems that arise. Beyond that, librarians must form a network of parents who believe in intellectual freedom and who are willing to contact school board members to oppose removing a book. It is essential that a network like this be in place prior to a crisis. Finally, school librarians should look to the lobbying techniques and strategies outlined in this book for school libraries to ensure that they are not caught off guard in this or any other area controlled by the school board.

Public libraries as well as school libraries occasionally face censorship problems when the governing body is put under pressure by vocal members of the community, special interest groups, or even one or more of their own members. In 1989 in Gwinnett County, Georgia, the public library board succumbed to public pressure and set up a card system for children to prohibit them from checking out dictionaries and certain materials under such classifications as science fiction and adult titles. The library board chair indicated that the board took this action to "pacify people."[41]

These kinds of public officials (most often appointed, sometimes elected) are hard to fight, because librarians are forced to battle the very individuals who hire and fire them. The school librarian faces a similar problem when the principal in a school decides to remove a book. Librarians have several options. As mentioned previously, a written selection policy approved by the school board may initially dissuade the principal from such a drastic action. Another way to handle this kind of situation is for the librarian to establish a support group in favor of an individual's right to select materials before the problem arises and let this group pressure the library board or the principal. When two community groups have diametrically opposed viewpoints, it is harder for the library board or principal to make a decision based on "pacifying people."

Other solutions exist. Obviously the most difficult way for librarians to approach the censorship problem is to fight their own board, especially if it means losing their job. At a time when jobs are hard to come by, this option is not one that many librarians are willing to take. Another solution is to work on an ongoing basis with your board regarding the issues of freedom to read and the age-old library tradition of protecting people's rights under the United States Constitution. If the library board is prepped and educated before a problem arises, the librarian will not have to fight it, and it will find the decision against censorship easy to make regardless of pressure by special interest groups.

Librarians may use many of the techniques in this book on their own library board, principal, or school board to facilitate understanding of censorship and the unique role libraries play in protecting a person's freedom to read and have access to information.

State Level

Perhaps more onerous than a local board's power to remove one book from the shelves in one institution is the lawmaking ability of state legislatures to require simultaneously all the libraries in the state to remove certain materials from their shelves. Pornography legislation is the most often-cited legislative problem against which librarians fight. Before I was a legislator, I testified as a librarian before a Wyoming State Senate Committee against the passage of a child pornography bill that was so broad it could have banned most movies with child actors from being shown in Wyoming. The committee basically ignored my comments and voted unanimously in favor of the legislation, which eventually died of its own accord. The newspaper story detailing my remarks made me feel uncomfortable at the time, however, since I was the only person opposing the legislation. After all, who is in favor of child pornography? Perhaps had an appropriate statewide lobbying network been in place, the committee would have paid more attention, and I would not have been alone in the hearing room.

Federal Level

Legislation at the national level is probably the hardest to fight and the most dangerous of all, because national legislation affects libraries throughout the United States. Many librarians find dealing with Congress abstract and hard to do. Their library budgets usually do not have an appropriation for federal lobbying, and their library boards often believe that problems can be solved at home.

The library world as a whole, however, has been successful in its challenge of the Child Protection and Obscenity Enforcement Act of 1988. The Freedom to Read Foundation of the American Library Association was joined by the American Booksellers Association and the Magazine Publishers' Association in a legal challenge to this law.[42] The court held unconstitutional the provisions that required publishers to keep records of the names, ages, and addresses of models who were used to depict sexual activity and that allowed police to seize material they deemed to be child pornography prior to a judicial determination that the material was illegal.[43]

Librarians must continue to fight and lobby for First Amendment rights because few groups in the United States are committed to protecting our constitutional rights in this area. It is often an unpopular area to protect because diverse and minority opinions are not always appreciated or tolerated by the majority.

Other Governmental Problems Affecting Libraries

Governmental problems needing political action from librarians are constant and unpredictable. The most unusual and recent effort of the United States government that librarians successfully fought was the FBI Library Awareness Program.

Other decisions made at the federal level that affect libraries include governmental policies on wage and price controls, copyright laws, the printing and distribution of government documents, and the reorganization of the Library of Congress, to name a few.[44] A list of federal legislation affecting libraries in just one year is extensive (see Table 2). The committee reports provide librarians with said information on the legislative intent of a particular bill, while the final public law number allows librarians to receive copies of the bill easily.

Most states prepared resolutions in anticipation of the 1991 White House Conference on Library and Information Services. Some of the preconference resolutions to Congress developed by the states on children's issues serve as an example of how much libraries look to Congress to help solve problems. Although these states may not currently be lobbying for the specific needs listed below, the issues represent the kind that Congress might face if the states decide that a particular issue merits national attention. Some of the resolutions are listed below.

1. *California:* Recommended federal legislation to provide technological equipment for school and public libraries to access information on a national network level.
2. *Minnesota:* Recommended federal legislation to fund school and public library demonstrations of intergenerational programs to provide services such as tutoring, leisure activities, hobbies, etc., for school children in collaboration with networks and private associations such as the American Association of Retired People.
3. *New York:* Recommended federal legislation to provide assistance for and incentives to library programs that help parents of preschool children develop needed parenting skills.
4. *Wisconsin:* Recommended federal legislation to provide categorical funding for school libraries.[45]

Table 2   Legislation of Interest to Librarians

101st Congress, 2nd Session Convened: January 23, 1990 Adjourned: October 28, 1990	House Indroduced	House Comm Rept. No.- H.Rept 101-	Senate Indroduced	Senate Comm Rept. No.- S.Rept 101-	Conf. Rept.- H.Rep 101-	Final pass.	Pub. Law-PL 101-
American Technology Preeminence Act	HR 4329	481	S 1191	159			
Americans With Disabilities Act	HR 2273	485	S 933	116	596	•	336
Arts and Humanities Endowments Reauthorization	HR 4825	566	S 2724	472			
Child Care	HR 3	190	S 5	17			
Civil Rights Act Amendments	HR 4000	644	S 2104	315	856	•	Veto
Copyright–computer software rental	HR 5498, 5316	735	S 198	265	None	•	650
Copyright–states' immunity	HR 3045	282	S 497	305	887	•	553
Copyright–unpublished works	HR 4263, 5498		S 2370				
Educational Equity and Excellence Act	HR 5115, 5932	570	S 695	136			
Family and Medical Leave Act	HR 770	28	S 345	77	None	•	Veto\
GPO Improvement Act	HR 3849						
Literacy Bills	HR 3123		S 1310	196			
Medical Library Assistance Act Reauthorization	HR 5661	869	S 2857	459			
National Agricultural Library	HR 3950	569	S 2830	357	916	•	624
National and Community Service Act	HR 4330	677	S 1430	176	893	•	610
National Research and Education Network	HR 3131		S 1067	387			
NREN–Department of Energy Bill			S 1976	377			
Omnibus Budget Reconciliation Act	HR 5835	881	S 3209	None	964	•	508
Paperwork Reduction Act Reauthorization	HR 3695	927	S 1742	487			
Permanent Paper and Recycling	HR 3094, 3735						
Permanent Paper Policy	HJRes 226	680	SJRes 57	None	None	•	423
Taxation–manuscript donations	HR 1427, 5081		S 262, 1503				
Teacher Recruitment and Training	HR 4130, 5115	570	S 1676	360			
Year of the Lifetime Reader	HJRes 571		SJRes 292				
Appropriations, FY 1991							
Agriculture	HR 5268	598	HR 5268	468	907	•	506
Commerce, State	HR 5021	537	HR 5021	515	909	•	515
Interior and Related Agencies	HR 5769	789	HR 5769	534	971	•	512
Labor-HHS-Education	HR 5257	591	HR 5257	516	908	•	517
Legislative Branch	HR 5399	648	S 3207	533	965	•	520
Treasury, Postal Service	HR 5241	589	HR 5241	411	906	•	509
VA, HUD, Independent Agencies	HR 5158	556	HR 5158	474	900	•	507

For free copies of bills, reports, and laws, write: House Document Room, B-18 Annex No. 2, Washington, DC 20515; Senate Document Room, B-04 Hart, Washington, DC 20510

Federal legislation affects libraries in many ways. With a little imagination and honed lobbying skills, librarians can start affecting and passing legislation of their own instead of primarily being reactive to legislation introduced by others.

Notes

1. Kathleen Molz Redmond, *The Federal Roles in Support of Public Library Services: An Overview* (Chicago: American Library Association, 1990), 9.

2. Ibid.

3. Ibid.

4. Ibid. An excellent chronology of changes to this legislation can be found on pages 10–12 of this booklet.

5. Eileen Cooke, American Library Association Washington Office.

6. U.S. Dept. of Education, Office of Library Programs, Office of Educational Research and Improvement, *Fact Sheet: Public Library Services, FY 1991* (Winter 1990–91).

7. U.S. Dept. of Education, Office of Library Programs, Office of Educational Research and Improvement, *Fact Sheet: Public Library Construction and Technology Enhancement, FY 1991* (Winter 1990–91).

8. U.S. Dept. of Education, Office of Library Programs, Office of Educational Research and Improvement, *Fact Sheet: Interlibrary Cooperation and Resource Sharing, FY 1991* (Winter 1990–91).

9. U.S. Dept. of Education, Office of Library Programs, Office of Educational Research and Improvement, *Fact Sheet: Library Services for Indian Tribes and Hawaiian Natives Program Basic Grants, FY 1991* (Winter 1990–91).

10. U.S. Dept. of Education, Office of Library Programs, Office of Educational Research and Improvement, *Fact Sheet: Foreign Language Materials Acquisition Program, FY 1991* (Winter 1990–91).

11. U.S. Dept. of Education, Office of Library Programs, Office of Educational Research and Improvement, *Fact Sheet: Library Literacy Program, FY 1991* (Winter 1990–91).

12. American Library Association Washington Office, Library Services and Construction Act Fact Sheet (Washington, D.C.: American Library Association, April 1991), 9–10.

13. Ibid., 10.

14. Ibid.

15. Ibid.

16. Redmond, *The Federal Roles in Support of Public Library Services*, 8.

17. Mary Jo Lynch, "F.S.C.S. and the Evaluation of L.S.C.A.," *Library Programs: Evaluating Federally Funded Public Library Programs* (Washington, D. C.: Govt. Print. Off., July 1990), 91.

18. Ibid., 95.

19. Kathleen Molz Redmond, *The Federal Roles in Support of Academic and Research Libraries* 3, quoting Alan Carter Smith, "The Higher Education Act, Title II-A: Its Impact on the Academic Library," *Library Trends* 24 (July 1975): 65.

20. Redmond, *The Federal Roles in Support of Academic and Research Libraries*, 4–5.

21. Ibid., 5.

22. U.S. Dept. of Education, Office of Library Programs, Office of Educational Research and Improvement, *Fact Sheet: Library Career Training Program, FY 1991* (Winter 1990–91).

23. Redmond, *The Federal Roles in Support of Academic and Research Libraries*, 6–7.

24. U.S. Dept. of Education, Office of Library Programs, Office of Educational Research and Improvement, *Fact Sheet: Strengthening Research Library Resources Program, FY 1991* (Winter 1990–91).

25. Redmond, *The Federal Roles in Support of Academic and Research Libraries*, 7–8, quoting Linda Loeb, "Federal Funds for Networking," *The Bottom Line* 4, no. 2 (1990); and U.S. Dept. of Education, Office of Library Programs, Office of Educational Research and Improvement, *Fact Sheet: College Library Technology and Cooperation Grants Program, FY 1991* (Winter 1990–91).

26. Redmond, *The Federal Roles in Support of Academic and Research Libraries*, 9–10.

27. Dianne McAfee Hopkins and Rebecca P. Butler, *The Federal Roles in Support of School Library Media Centers* (Chicago: American Library Association, 1991), 5–6.

28. Ibid., 8.

29. Ibid., 8; Louise Sutherland, "School Library Legislation at the Federal Level," *Library Trends* (October 1970): 199.

30. Hopkins and Butler, *The Federal Roles in Support of School Library Media Centers*, 9.

31. Ibid., 11–12.

32. Ibid., 13.

33. Ibid., 13–14.

34. Ibid., 15, quoting Wayne Clifton Riddle, *Federal Assistance to Libraries: Current Programs and Issues, CRS Report for Congress* (Washington, D.C.: Congressional Research Service, Library of Congress, 1990), 20.

35. Ibid., 20.

36. Contact Eileen Cooke, American Library Association, Washington Office, (202) 547-4440.

37. George Alderson and Everett Sentman, *How You Can Influence Congress: The Complete Handbook for the Citizen Lobbyist* (New York: E. P. Dutton, 1979); David Shavit, *Federal Aid and State Library Agencies: Federal Policy Implementation* (Westport, Conn.: Greenwood Press, 1985); Eileen Cooke, "Persuading Politicians to Support U.S. Libraries," *The Role of Library Associations as Effective Pressure Groups for Political Action*, IFLA Professional Reports 14 (1987); Harold B. Shill, "Librarians Fight Zero-funding of Federal Programs," *West Virginia Libraries* 38, no. 2 (Summer 1983): 23–27; Art Plotnik, Mary Jane McKinven, Edith McCormick, Barbara Jacobs, Elizabeth Mitchell, and John Wilkins, "Washington Library Power: Who Has It, and How It Works for You," *American Libraries* 6, no. 11 (December 1975): 647–674.

38. Office for Intellectual Freedom, *Intellectual Freedom Manual* (Chicago: American Library Association, 1974).

39. Bohdan Szuchewycz, "New Right Publications: A Survey of Public and Academic Libraries in Metropolitan Toronto," *Canadian Library Journal* 47 (February 1990): 17.

40. Note the father who convinced the school board to declare Dr. Seuss's Book, *The Lorax*, "unsuitable" in Laytonville, California, because he claimed it mocked the timber industry. Bertha M. Cheatham, "A Fight for Rights: The Year In Review," *School Library Journal* 35 (December, 1989): 30.

41. Ibid.

42. Ibid.

43. Ibid.

44. Hannah D. Atkins, "Impact of Governmental Politics and Economics on Library Information Services: A View From the Inside," *Special Libraries* 70 (November 1979): 459.

45. From "Examples of White House Preconference Resolutions and Recommendations Concerning Library Services for Children and Young Adults," prepared by the division of the American Library Association whose members provide resources and services for children and young adults in school and public libraries, and sent to all White House Conference on Library and Information Services delegates and alternates.

2

The Basics of Lobbying

The Necessity of Lobbying

In order to continue to survive, libraries of all sizes and kinds must adapt themselves to our changing environment, including the political environment. For too long librarians have felt they must be apolitical and maintain an apolitical bias.[1] By being politically passive, librarians have handed over all power affecting their libraries to the decision makers. By not taking political positions, librarians are not apolitical; they simply have made a political decision to be inactive.[2] This kind of decision often leads to libraries' being left off the decision makers' priority lists. Even other entities recognize and lament the library's "long-standing tradition of aloofness from city hall and its occupants," by which the library has cut itself out of local political activity and consequently "has seriously deterred recognition of its program and the financing end to carry it out."[3] As one author queried, if someone knocked on your door and told you that he was your new neighbor and that he had "the authority to increase your taxes, reduce your education budget, and imperil your health and safety," wouldn't you want to get to know this person?[4]

An initial question is, what is lobbying? Authors disagree on the precise definition of lobbying but usually agree that it carries negative connotations. In the Pennsylvania Trustee Handbook, lobbying is defined as a form of communication and the process of expressing opinions to the decision makers and pushing those opinions.[5] Alice Ihrig says lobbying is the process of expressing needs to decision makers, and although lobbying is not "of suspect legality," it sometimes requires registering as a lobbyist.[6] Mary J. LeMessurier states that lobbying is interaction with politicians to secure specific objectives at an appropriate point in the legislative, policy-making, or budget process. She then states that lobbying is not advocacy, which she defines as the deliberate, sustained effort to raise awareness on a topic; and it is not public relations, the promotion of the group itself.[7] Lobbying is close to advocacy, however, according to the California Trustee Handbook. It defines advocacy as "speaking in favor; public recommendation; support," and lobbying as trying "to influence legislators" by approaching them in the halls or lobby of the capitol building as they exit.[8] Lobbying is also close to public relations, since lobbyists use many of the techniques associated with public relations, and decision makers are members of the public. However, because of the distinctly specialized role of decision makers, the effort is more accurately described as "governance relations," and using governance relations is the essence of lobbying. The California handbook perhaps best summarizes lobbying when it states that "the lines between advocacy, working relationship with local officials, and public/community relations . . . overlap," but that the important thing is "doing them all and doing them well, no matter by what name they are called."[9]

Over the years lobbying has received bad press when both elected officials and lobbyists abuse it. Most elected officials, however, do not consider lobbying bad. Lobbyists provide information and education on a topic about which the decision maker may not be fully informed. For the purposes of this book, lobbying will mean any kind of effort—whether it is short-term or long-term, one interaction or a thousand. It can be initiated purposefully by an individual, group of individuals, or an organization in order to attain a goal, or it may arise inadvertently as a result of a spontaneous interaction that results in a change in thought or attitude by an elected official.

No longer can libraries expect to be funded year after year at the same level because they are inherently good. Librarians must establish a thoughtful lobbying effort to educate decision makers about the library's needs so that libraries do not continue to take a back seat to other government-funded agencies or departments. Librarians need to recognize that they are competing with a variety of new public demands, such as additional funding for education to meet the needs of sophisticated day-care and latchkey children or for such environmental efforts as hazardous waste cleanup. In addition, libraries continue to be pitted against the old competitors—sheriff's offices, school football teams, and faculty payrolls—for a share of the shrinking public tax pie. As part of the lobbying effort, librarians must develop a broad community base through public service and cultivate a strong relationship between the library and key individuals in the community.[10] These people can then help put the pressure on the appropriate decision makers to maintain or increase funding for libraries.

Increasingly, librarians must also address new, nonbudgetary political problems that require lobbying efforts. At the state level, for example, in the past three years, the Wyoming legislature has passed or considered legislation regarding the following issues that affect all kinds of libraries in the state tremendously: (1) combining the state library with the University of Wyoming library, basically eliminating the state library altogether; (2) combining the state library's collections of government documents with the university's government documents division; (3) building a new state library; (4) creating authorization for library districts; and (5) adding library patron files to the confidentiality law. Librarians in every state need to be ready to act when an unexpected detrimental bill is introduced. Conversely, librarians need to be a driving force behind legislation they want passed, whether it is at the national, state, or local level.

The Fruits of Lobbying

Although many librarians might disagree, lobbying is one of the most important duties of every library director. Further, every individual who works in a library, from the janitor to the cataloger, serves as an ongoing library lobbyist in one form or another. Lobbying should therefore be a planned part of a library's goals and objectives, and employees should be trained to recognize their important role in this area.

The fruits of lobbying are many. A few of the benefits include: (1) increasing library funding; (2) creating goodwill with the public, who in turn puts pressure on the decision makers at the appropriate time; (3) avoiding onerous and uninformed, albeit well-intentioned, efforts by decision makers; and (4) ensuring an "ear" for a problem when necessary. Although librarians must make many in-house decisions, they also need to anticipate and influence any decisions made by others that will directly affect them. Planning an ongoing lobbying effort, even during those years when no problems exist, is time well spent.

What, Me Lobby? Or, The Plight of the Citizen-Lobbyist

A lobbyist does not necessarily wear an official badge, register with the appropriate authority, or call herself or himself a lobbyist. A person becomes a citizen-lobbyist when she or he interacts with a decision maker and makes a comment concerning an issue the official can affect. Deborah Miller puts it succinctly: "There are over 11 million lobbyists in Illinois, but only 350 or so are registered with the secretary of state. To lobby is to try to influence public officials, something every citizen does at one time or another. . . . "[11] Librarians consequently need to interact thoughtfully with the individuals who have the power to make major decisions about their library. Every personal contact is important. Librarians should take advantage of any time spent with decision makers to communicate their message effectively.

Citizen-lobbying can even happen unintentionally. Individuals need to be aware that when they interact with a public official they may be influencing that person's opinion on something whether they mean to or not. Almost without exception, every interaction with a legislator is lobbying, inadvertent or intentional. Elected officials rarely stop thinking about their responsibilities and ways to solve problems. Talking to one is not like talking to a "normal" human being, even if the elected official is your best friend. After only a short while as an elected official, the world changes into problems and situations the elected official can or cannot affect.

Even off-the-cuff statements in a grocery store or elsewhere that would have been hardly noteworthy before election take on new significance for an elected official. For example, when a library patron discusses casually with a county commissioner the terrible physical condition of a library, the county commissioner has a hard time not thinking about it as a problem which he or she must face at some point. The commissioner automatically puts on a decision maker's hat and listens carefully to what the friend is saying.

Indeed, most people consider an elected individual "fair game" for discussing problems, and hearing complaints is certainly part of the official's responsibilities. The interaction need not take place in the capitol building or in the city or county complex. Lobbying can take place anywhere and under the most unlikely circumstances. I have been lobbied in precarious positions during doctor's examinations.

When I attended an art reception with a friend, it took forty-five minutes to travel from the front door to the punch bowl because of the number of people who wanted to discuss problems. Some of the people were quite angry about the issues concerning them. When I indicated to my friend that this was a common occurrence, she was aghast and stated that she did not want to ever run for office. A fellow senator commented to me that he made a mistake by stopping at the first reservoir when he went fishing last summer. He never got a chance to throw a line into the water because so many people stopped to discuss issues with him. Decision makers expect this kind of constant contact with constituents and encourage it. Constituents (library supporters, take note!) need to realize that legislators consider many interactions with them as lobbying. Citizen-lobbyists should know what they want to communicate and do it thoughtfully, even when it is an unexpected interaction. Be careful not to invade decision makers' privacy or to approach them unnecessarily at a social event. Although they expect such interruptions, they enjoy time away from their job.

A final note is that when citizens lobby their elected officials as library trustees, concerned library citizens, friends of the library, etc., they carry a lot more weight than the paid lobbyists at the capitol. A single person can influence an elected official tremendously, since often a legislator hears only from a handful of individuals on any given topic. When that person speaks from his or her heart about a subject, rather than speaking for pay on behalf of any organization, the elected official recognizes that the person is speaking for many others in the community and listens carefully.

Notes

1. Hannah D. Atkins, "Impact of Governmental Politics and Economics on Library Information Services; A View from the Inside," *Special Libraries* 70 (November 1979): 457.

2. Ibid.

3. Betty Bay, ed., *Trustee Tool Kit for Library Leadership* (Sacramento, California State Library, 1987), 173, quoting *Local Public Library Administration*, the International City Managers' Association text on libraries.

4. Marc Caplan, *Ralph Nader Presents a Citizens' Guide to Lobbying* (New York: Dembner Enterprises Corporation, 1983), 7.

5. *A Handbook for Public Library Trustees* (Harrisburg: Pennslyvania State Library, 1989), 35.

6. Alice Ihrig, "Lobbying," in *Funding Alternatives for Libraries*, eds. Patricia Senn Breivik and E. Burr Gibson (Chicago: American Library Association, 1979), 94.

7. Mary J. LeMessurier, "Successful Lobbying Techniques," *Canadian Library Journal* 44 (August 1977: 231.

8. Bay, *Trustee Tool Kit for Library Leadership*, 194.

9. Ibid.

10. Leonard H. Frieser, "Fundraising and the Meaning of Public Support," *Library Journal* 110 (12 June 1985): 29–31.

11. Deborah Miller, "The Librarian/Trustee as Successful Lobbyist," *Trustee Handbook* (Montgomery: Alabama Public Library Service, 1984), 58.

3

Key Players Who Lobby

The Library Director

Who is one of the most important players in the day-to-day library lobbying process? The library director, or whoever the library director appoints as the liaison between the library and the legislative body, is key to any lobbying efforts. Part of every library director's role, whether in a school library, a public library, or a special library, is to be politically active. Political action means joining clubs and organizations within the community; it means serving as the chair of the United Way drive; it means getting to know the members of the funding bodies personally when possible and gaining their trust; it means educating and communicating with those individuals so that they understand the library's problems and needs before a crisis occurs; it means developing a long-term plan to lobby the appropriate sources; and it means educating and training staff members to deal effectively with political issues identified in the library's long-term plan.

The list of political responsibilities continues. The best library-director lobbyist will not stay within the walls of the library but will instead become well-known and well-liked in the community. A good library director can be the best asset the library has, and the library board should consider lobbying part of the administrative duties of the library director. The money, goodwill and exposure that the library will reap through the efforts of a politically astute librarian are well worth the investment of time the librarian makes.

The Library Employee, Volunteer, Board Member, and Others

All individuals associated with a library serve as lobbyists for that library. This group includes library employees, spouses of library employees, friends of the library, library board members, library volunteers, and any other individual even remotely associated with a library, especially in a small town. Unfortunately, the public at large and many decision makers are unable to distinguish among the various groups and their responsibilities. Consequently, volunteers are sometimes asked important questions by the decision makers yet are insufficiently trained to provide full answers. More important, individuals associated with the library are judged by their manner and activities even when they are not working in their capacity as an employee or volunteer. The library director needs to know and understand the impact that all people associated with the library may have, especially around budget time or when the legislature is in session.

Library directors need to train staff, volunteers, friends, and board members to handle political questions, and even apolitical questions that may be important to the individual asking. For example, if a library volunteer is asked why the library reduced its hours, that volunteer must know the answer, or at the very least know that he or she should take the name and phone number of the person asking and have the library director (or the appropriate library personnel) contact the questioner. Training of this sort can help prevent ramifications that an incorrect or ignorant answer might have on the library in the long run.

Everyday interaction between library "folks" and others requires a thoughtful training and updating program by the library director or appropriate staff member. The average citizen does not distinguish among the different individuals associated with a library—everyone is a "librarian."

The Professional Library Lobbyist

The professional lobbyist has two roles. The first is to provide information to local libraries or library systems about legislation, amendments, public hearings, etc., affecting libraries so that a library legislative network can be activated. Each librarian can then contact representatives, aldermen and alderwomen, or senators from his or her district. The second role of a lobbyist is to gain the trust of the decision makers and provide them with information about libraries and any pending legislation sponsored, supported, or opposed by libraries. A lobbyist can be counted on to send information both ways—back to the librarians and on to the legislator.

Lobbyist for a Library Association

A state library association should hire a trained individual, either full- or part-time, who can stay at the state capital during crucial periods, "watchdog" (monitor) legislation, and contact the appropriate individuals. Frequently, without a lobbyist, librarians find themselves in the position of discovering a bill that affects them after it is too late to do anything about it. The process moves too quickly to leave lobbying solely to volunteers or even to diligent librarians who must also maintain their normal library responsibilities during legislative sessions. Even if a lobbyist is hired, librarians cannot leave the lobbying responsibility solely to the lobbyist. Individual legislative committees headed by librarians throughout the state and statewide library legislative networks are still essential to any lobbying effort. Passing or killing library legislation requires extensive statewide lobbying.

A lobbyist at the capital ensures that librarians will be aware of important events during a fast-paced legislative session. States have different policies regarding public hearings and public notification of bill titles or content. Legislators are under no obligation to support a bill or an amendment of any kind, and they need not notify the people it affects. In fact, most legislators must deal with so many bills that it would be impossible for them to call interested individuals on every bill. Many certainly try to call constituents on major bills, but the process moves too quickly in many states to allow this kind of communication consistently. The lobbyist will fill this gap and notify appropriate contact persons in the state or at the state library about these bills.

Further, even if a librarian scans all the bills introduced as the session starts and finds none that affect libraries, unexpected legislation can appear suddenly out of nowhere. Legislators have a cutoff deadline for introducing bills, but up until that date "throwing a bill into the hopper" is acceptable. Many people have strange notions about libraries, but if a person with a strange notion about libraries is also a legislator introducing a bill that could seriously affect libraries, then librarians must be able to alert the library world immediately. A library lobbyist will know about a new onerous (or beneficial) bill immediately upon introduction and will contact the appropriate individuals throughout the state.

A lobbyist is also critical to successful funding for the state library. State library budgets affect the level of services local libraries throughout the state receive. I have heard more than one legislator question the need for a state library at all. In addition, the laws of many states provide for distribution of state money to local libraries in the form of programs such as state aid to public libraries. The appropriate legislative funding committee can cut a state library's budget or add footnotes affecting library funding to a general governmental budget bill. Such decisions represent a potential crisis for the state library as well as for libraries statewide, and someone needs to alert the library community immediately. Some state libraries are allowed to sound the alarm. Other state library personnel are under a "gag order" prohibiting them from acting as a lobbyist for the state. A state library association and a state library can work together in such a situation to ensure that the librarians in the state are not "blind sided" by a bill or an amendment, although they must be careful that the state library not disobey its orders to stay out of the political process. A professional lobbyist hired by the state library association could notify the appropriate parties without the state library's involvement.

Finally, a lobbyist at the state level can keep track of public hearings on bills that are moving through the legislative process. Public hearings are often good forums for a librarian's input into a bill. However, some states do not require that such meetings be announced more than twenty-four hours in advance, or that the announcement be placed anywhere but at the state capitol. In such a situation, a skilled lobbyist knows to notify the appropriate individuals quickly when a notice for a hearing is posted. Without a person to watch legislation closely, librarians may lose some precious opportunities to influence legislation affecting them.

Lobbyist for Larger Public Library or System

The large public library may question whether it should hire an official lobbyist to represent the library. Most larger public libraries or library systems do not need to hire a lobbyist to communicate with the local funding body. Personal contacts among the librarian, the trustees, and the elected officials at the local level, even in a larger city, are easier than at the state level. Local elected officials expect this kind of personal interaction. The library director and trustees need to develop working relationships with the local elected officials regarding such matters as the budget, tax issues, local ordinances, etc., and keep in relatively close touch with the officials through meetings, letters, and personal contact. They must educate local decision makers about potential library legislation and interact with them enough to feel comfortable asking them to introduce an ordinance on behalf of the library. An intervening lobbyist could be helpful if the governing body is extremely active and if no library representative has been able to lay the groundwork for a good relationship. A lobbyist could also be helpful if a major library system exists and it needs a coordinated lobbying effort.

However, a paid lobbyist can also be detrimental to the library's efforts. The elected officials deciding on a budget for a public library may believe that if the library can afford to hire a lobbyist, it certainly does not need additional funding from the county or the city. To avoid the lucrative budget arguments, the Friends of the Library could pay for lobbying efforts on behalf of a large library; or in the case of a library system, part of the dues from each library could pay for a lobbyist. The lobbyist in those situations must let the elected officials know who is paying his or her salary. Another problem with a paid lobbyist is that some decision makers consider lobbyists less important than the library trustees or director and feel that the library representatives are snubbing them by sending a hired gun.

Librarians from larger libraries need to evaluate their own situation and elected officials and weigh the pros and cons before deciding to hire a lobbyist.

Communication Types and Tips

Throughout the rest of this book, we will follow the lobbying adventures of Ruth Poe, director of the mythical Elksberg Public Library. She wants the legislature to pass a bill to create library districts. The number of the bill for which she is lobbying is Senate File 102. If passed, the bill would create optional library districts that allow citizens in any county in the state to tax themselves for library services. She will do some things right and some things wrong in her lobbying effort. Everyone makes mistakes—even the veteran lobbyist!

Written Communication

Letters

As simple as it may sound, a thoughtful, handwritten letter from a constituent is one of the most effective lobbying tools anyone can use.

February 17, 1992

The Honorable John Vinich
P. O. Box 248
Elksburg, WY 82070

Dear Senator Vinich:

     I am the new librarian at Elksburg Public Library. I know you are facing tough issues this year at the Capitol, but I would appreciate it greatly if you would support full funding for the State Library.

     It provides many services to public libraries around the state including consulting, central purchasing, distribution of LSCA grants and continuing education. It gives the state money through cooperative interlibrary loan efforts. The State Library is a bargain! Please support its budget!

                                    Sincerely,
                                    Ruth Poe
                                    Director

A sincere handwritten message is an effective tool.

Note, however, that if your regular handwriting is terrible, take the time to write clearly. A decision makers will attempt to read bad writing but will not waste time if a letter is impossible to decipher.

Decision makers receive a tremendous amount of written information from constituents and from special interest groups. The letters that are read and answered are those that show personal, individualized effort. A library can coordinate a writing campaign with

March 14, 1991

The Honorable John Vinich
P.O. Box 248
Elksburg, WY 82070

PUBLIC LIBRARY

Dear Senator Vinich:

The Wyoming Library Association is supporting a patron
privacy bill, and I would appreciate your support on it. Currently
there is a disagreement among professionals in the state whether
library records fall under the Public Records Act or whether
they are more akin to public utility records and are therefore
private. This legislation would resolve the issue so that librarians
will know how to handle requests by third parties to look at
library records.

If this bill passes, it would protect the patron's right to
privacy, it would provide legal standing for current library policy
throughout the state, and it would protect librarians and library
board members when following their own policies.

I would be glad to answer questions if you have any. Please
feel free to give me a call at the above number. Thank you so
much for consideration of this bill and the issues involved.

Sincerely,

Ruth Poe, Director
Elksburg Public Library

As long as it appears individualized, a personal typewritten
letter is also effective.

the Friends of the Library. Many libraries have done so. However,
when these campaigns are organized, librarians must stress to the
volunteers the importance of writing the letter in their own words.
The same message worded differently in each letter is effective.

A photocopied message or dozens of letters with the same three
points showing no thought or understanding of an issue are ineffective. Many decision makers will often not bother answering letters
in which the writers appear to have copied a predetermined, uniform message.

An individualized typed letter from a concerned citizen can be nearly as effective as a handwritten letter. However, home computers can take away some of the effectiveness of an individual's typewritten letter when the letter looks as if it has been mass-produced and sent to every decision maker. To counteract this impression, do not justify the margins on a computer letter, and try to make the letter as personal and anecdotally related to the decision maker as possible. For instance, include a comment about meeting the legislator (if you did), or liking his or her comments in committee or during a particular meeting. Do not start the letter with a generic "Dear Legislator."

May 14, 1991

The Honorable John Vinich
P. O. Box 248
Elksburg, WY 82070

PUBLIC LIBRARY

Dear Senator Vinich:

   This is just a short note to let you know how pleased I was to meet you when you spoke recently to the League of Women Voters about reapportionment of the state and how the new census figures will affect our county. Your presentation was excellent, and I appreciated hearing your comments on this subject. I wrote you a couple of letters earlier this year and was pleased to be able to listen to you in person.
   As you may recall, I am the director of the Elksburg Public Library. Several librarians and I see a need for library districts in the state and would like to discuss this with you at your convenience. I will be in touch soon in order to arrange a time to meet with you.
   Thanks again for sharing your expertise with us. I look forward to talking with you again.

Sincerely,

Ruth Poe, Director
Elksburg Public Library

Petitions

A petition is another type of written communication. A petition will often start with, "We, the undersigned constituents of your district, request that . . . ," or "ask you to vote in favor of . . . ," etc. People then sign underneath the typewritten body of the petition.

A petition is not an extremely effective method of communication, but if it is used, here are some basic tips. A petition has little impact if the decision maker cannot read the signatures. Perhaps the signatory is a person whom the decision maker respects and listens to. If the writing is illegible, the power of that person's name is lost. To resolve this issue, provide a place for a printed name next to the place for the signature, as in the sample below. Many individuals have illegible signatures, and it is extremely frustrating for the decision maker not to be able to read names on a petition. When writing to a petitioner, I have sometimes just cut out an illegible signature from a petition and pasted it on a mailing envelope instead of trying to guess what the name was.

Also make sure that there is a place for the signatory's address. Decision makers often want to communicate with the individuals on the petition, but if they do not have the addresses, very few have the time or staff to look them up. Addresses also give additional information to the decision maker about whether the concerns all are from the same neighborhood or precinct or spread through diverse locales. Elected officials usually like to be responsive to their constituents. Give them the chance by including the addresses. In addition, if a decision maker has to form an opinion and write a response, the problem or issue becomes more ingrained in his or her head than if the person simply reads the petition and tosses it for lack of information.

Name (Printed)	Name (Signature)	Address	City	Phone

1. _____
2. _____
3. _____
4. _____
5. _____
6. _____
etc.

Good form for a petition

Brochures and Information Sheets

Another type of written communication is an informational brochure, flyer, or information sheet. This document can either focus on a particular issue the library is advocating or opposing or provide general information on the library and its needs. A decision maker will often keep a document containing specific information that can be used for debate or for underscoring the decision maker's point of view. A brochure containing general information that can be obtained again easily will probably hit the waste basket instead of the desk. If the document is not done well, the decision maker may disregard it, and it will have been a waste of the library's time. Think of this document as the representative of your library. Put your best foot forward.

The library has to determine exactly what it wants to communicate and then select an appropriate format. Because of the vast amount of information a decision maker receives, any library publication must be eye-catching, informative, concise, and important.

Several excellent books are available on how to make effective brochures.[1] Brochures are especially useful when lobbying for a budget since budget information is hard to follow. A brochure can provide a division or separation of categories or figures to make the budget easier to understand.

If the librarian chooses an information sheet, a one-page sheet with captions and space between paragraphs will likely be read. A closely spaced, small-lettered, hard-to-read sheet is ineffective.

Personal Notes

An effective lobbying method in written form was used during the 1991 Wyoming legislative session. A group advocating a victim's rights bill left a short note on every legislator's desk daily. It was a brightly colored 3 × 5 sheet of paper folded in two with the legislator's name hand-printed on the outside. The message on the inside was short: "Today is the first (second, third, etc.) reading of House Bill #____. Thanks so much for your continued support." The note was signed by an individual involved with the lobbying process. It was simple and effective, an easy to-read reminder of the bill and its import. In addition, it also served as a personal thank-you note for three days running. After final passage of the bill, each legislator received an additional thank-you note in the same format. Many city ordinances require multiple readings and hearings, and this same technique could be adapted to fit a local library's needs.

Telegrams

Telegrams can be effective, but if the sender is in the same city as the legislature or governing body, decision makers may wonder why the person did not send a letter or call instead to save money. And if all decision makers in the body receive a telegram at the same time in the same room, they may be unimpressed because it was nothing special. However, if a "swing vote" decision maker receives a telegram, that person may feel flattered or singled out, and the effort could pay off. The key is timing and selectivity.

Faxes

With the advent of the fax, telegrams may become extinct. How effective is a fax to a decision maker? It can be effective because of its speed, especially if the decision maker has a fax machine in his or her office. For example, if a decision maker needs current statistics from a library in another part of the state during a budget session, the librarian can fax that information immediately so it can be distributed to the governing body as it deliberates on the issue. Until every person has a fax machine, however, faxes can cause an occasional problem. During one legislative session I received an unsolicited fax from someone in another part of the state. The fax was sent through a commercial copying center. A couple of weeks later, I received a bill from the copying center for the fax transaction, which I had not, of course, initiated or authorized. Sending a fax "collect" is definitely a poor lobbying technique and should be avoided. Be aware also that faxes are not placed in envelopes and that anyone can (and will) read your message given the chance. Many people consider faxes fair game.

Thank-You Notes

Finally, the most important written document a library supporter can send to a decision maker is a thank-you note. The lobbyist should see that thank-you notes are written to the appropriate legislators following each legislative activity to keep the decision makers interested.

Although this suggestion may sound elementary and trite, few people actually take the time to write thank-you notes to their politicians. Politicians are not generally well-liked, and they receive much public scorn. Even some librarians are publicly critical of legislators.[2] In any case, avoid the temptation to criticize, and instead write a thank-you note. Legislators enjoy receiving them, and they are effective. Every day, politicians face persons who are angry or want something from them. A short note thanking them for their support on something is a pleasant change that sticks in the decision makers' minds. Library supporters could effectively lobby decision makers by sending them dozens of thank-you notes after a vote or a good decision. What would they be lobbying for? The next library vote, whatever that may be!

Communicating by Phone

Individual Calling

Calling decision makers can be very effective under certain circumstances. Timing of calls is very important. Librarians should call decision makers immediately before a vote is taken on a particular bill or amendment affecting libraries. Decision makers receive many calls too late to affect their vote. They are frustrated when this happens, especially if the caller provided information which would have changed the decision makers' perspectives on the issue. Calling at the appropriate time, however, is difficult, because in many legislatures a bill moves quickly and unpredictably. Many legislatures have a number to call to determine the status of a bill. Individuals can even call the assembly, house, or senate chambers and ask what is being debated, but it is not always easy to get the information needed to coordinate calls with the hearing of the bills.

Calling Tree

A calling tree or network can be extremely effective. Commonly the person who is watchdogging an ordinance or bill calls a committee of callers (usually five), each of whom then calls an additional five, who then call their city council member or county supervisor. Although the tree can be put into action relatively quickly, there are several pitfalls to avoid in such an effort.

First, the most difficult aspect of this effort is educating the caller about the information or message the caller is supposed to relay to the decision maker. If the participants are not careful, the lobbying turns into a game of "Secret" in which one person in a circle whispers a secret to the next, who whispers the secret to the next, and so on until the message goes around the room. The message is always unclear at the end of the cycle. When a lobbying effort turns into a game of "Secret," the results can be disastrous. More than once I have heard a senator say that he received ten calls on one amendment the previous evening. He then tells the senate the messages he received and the questions he asked the callers. Invariably, only one or two callers could answer the questions that he asked, even though the questions were usually simple and straightforward regarding the content of the bill or amendment being advocated by the caller. He then opines to the senate that probably all the other legislators also received ten calls the previous evening (which we usually did), and that although the callers were well-intentioned, they were uninformed and the senators should not use the number of calls as a basis for making a decision. This strategy is an effective diffusion of the impact of a calling tree. To counteract this diffusion, make sure all callers are organized and well-informed about the law or budget in question. If the callers are not knowledgeable, a better strategy is to have one or two individuals who have significant facts to share with decision makers handle the calling. Two informed calls are more effective than two dozen calls made without sufficient background, however sincere the callers might be. The key is to know the difference between the two kinds of calls and when to encourage mass participation and when to encourage well-placed calls to a few by a few.

Telephone Hotlines

A simple "yes" or "no" vote by phone is effective when a telephone "hotline" to the legislature exists and people are encouraged to call and register a vote. Librarians and friends should take advantage of this kind of setup and should call often! However, calling a decision maker without speaking to him or her is less effective than writing a letter. A voter hotline can result in a page of names with "yes" and "no" votes, but a page of names with 200 calls on it does not have the same impact as a pile of 200 letters demanding answers.

Telephone Etiquette

You should always identify yourself immediately by name and city, county, or district, if applicable, and offer a short sentence on the issue you want to discuss. For example, "Hello, Supervisor Schmich, this is Cambria Lang from precinct 19. I'm calling to discuss the library ordinance with you." Immediately after that, ask the decision maker if this is a good time to talk or if you should call back. Although you run the risk of losing your one chance to talk, the decision maker appreciates your courtesy and thoughtfulness and will consider positively your statement about the library even if you never get a chance to deliver your message. Politicians tolerate and expect calls while they are in the middle of dinner, on the way to the shower, or in bed at night. The caller who actually asks if it is a good time to talk is such a refreshing change that the politician will usually return the call if the timing was bad.

Obviously, a decision maker does not answer the phone personally if he or she has a staff or secretary to screen calls or to run interference. In that case, get to know the secretary by name and develop an amicable relationship with that person. Getting by the gatekeeper is sometimes the hardest part of an interaction with an elected official. How many times have your messages been ignored? Persistence helps, but developing personal relationships with the right individuals goes even further in getting through.

Once you have a decision maker's ear, be concise, polite, and short-winded. Know what you want to say before you call. Do not leave to chance anything you could easily have thought out before the call. Thank the decision maker for his or her time and leave a number in case the decision maker has questions for you later.

Calling is more effective with some decision makers than with others. If possible, find out whether the person you are trying to influence is more auditory or visual. Determine early how a decision maker learns so that the library can use that method regularly. Some individuals will remember better if they see a message in writing rather than hear it over the phone. Those who like information in writing will often request a copy of an oral presentation you just made or ask you to write them a letter stating the issues you just discussed on the phone. After interacting with the governing officials over a period of time, the librarian will be able to determine the decision maker's preference. You might even ask if they have a preference. This information should be included in the file the library has developed on the decision maker.

Personal Contact

Generally

Librarians can meet personally with city council members or county supervisors in a number of ways. They can set up meetings at the decision maker's office or the library; they can invite the decision maker to participate in or attend library functions; or they can invite the decision maker to a meal or a reception. Official contact with decision makers to discuss library needs, however, must be systematic, timely, and continuous to be most effective. Year-round interaction is recommended, even if the library does not have any specific burning issues.[3]

Introductory Meeting

An introductory meeting is valuable if the librarian is new, the decision maker is new, or if this is the first time the library has become politically active. A get-acquainted lunch with each member of the city council or county board may take a while to set up and cost a few dollars, but the payback is well worth the effort. In addition, a restaurant is a neutral area, so that the librarian and the decision maker are on an equal footing. If an individual luncheon cannot be arranged, a short visit to the official's office to get acquainted is a good substitute. If you meet in the decision maker's office, however, the official may not be able to take off his or her "power" hat, and consequently you may not make as much of an impression.

Members of the governing body should have the opportunity to interact informally with librarians and trustees before the librarian requests anything from the decision makers.[4] The decision makers appreciate meeting with librarians without an official agenda or request—something that does not happen very often.

It is good for the elected official to know the librarian so that: (1) stereotyped images are avoided; (2) if problems or questions about the library arise, the decision maker knows whom to call; and (3) if the librarian attends the funding body meetings, the decision makers recognize him or her in the audience.

A local elected official is impressed by an interested librarian or trustee. According to studies cited later in this chapter, librarians are not often politically involved. When a librarian contacts an elected official and it is the first time the official has ever seen any initiative on the part of the library, the decision maker will be impressed.

June 23, 1991

The Honorable John Vinich
P. O. Box 248
Elksburg, WY 82070

PUBLIC LIBRARY

Dear Senator Vinich:

The chair of my library board and I would like to take you to lunch sometime during the next two weeks if you are available. We thought that since you are between sessions that this might be a good time for us to get better acquainted with you.

Although as I mentioned to you in my letter of last month, we are interested in a library district bill, at this time we have not had the opportunity to coalesce these thoughts. Instead, we would be delighted to have the opportunity just to meet with you informally at lunch.

Our preferred date is June 30 at noon. However, we can meet with you at your convenience. I will call you in the next couple of days to see if we can arrange a mutually convenient time.

I will talk with you soon.

Sincerely,

Ruth Poe, Director
Elksburg County Library

An introductory meeting with no formal agenda is a good idea.

On the other hand, if the former library director was politically active and the new librarian does not contact the local officials, the governing body may believe that the new librarian's policy is one of not getting involved. In any case, getting to know on a personal basis the local officials in charge of distributing tax dollars is an extremely effective method of lobbying.

If the reader remembers only one thing from this book, it should be the recommendation to develop personal relationships with decision makers. Insurance sales representatives are most successful in selling their product on their sixth try. This book will mention developing a good relationship at least six times with the hope that librarians will finally take note and start nurturing a relationship with their elected officials!

Meetings on Decision Makers' Turf

When the librarian and trustee are ready for more formal lobbying, they should make an official appointment with the decision maker to discuss the bill or referendum on which the library is working. The librarian should focus the meeting on a specific issue that the decision maker can affect. This meeting should be set up well in advance so that the librarians are not in the heat of panic over an impending decision and decision makers will have time to prepare for the meeting. Before such a meeting, the librarian should send to the decision maker a summary and important documentation on the issue. The decision maker will then not be embarrassed because he or she lacks background knowledge, and the decision maker will have a chance to prepare questions for the librarian and the trustee.

August 15, 1991

The Honorable John Vinich
P. O. Box 248
Elksburg, WY 82070

PUBLIC LIBRARY

Dear Senator Vinich:

I want to thank you again for having lunch with us in June. Both William and I enjoyed it very much. I hope that your trip to Chicago was as gratifying and fun as you expected it to be. Certainly, you must have been prepared for the real "windy city" given the weather we experienced here in late June! Also, I appreciated your comments about how to organize my thoughts on library district legislation. William asked me to send you his best regards.

As per your suggestion, I have spent the last two months working with librarians around the state to gain a consensus about what we think would be important in a library district bill. I would like to meet with you to discuss these elements and to get your opinion as to the feasibility of such a plan. Are you available for about an hour sometime during the next two weeks? I would be glad to meet with you wherever and whenever is most convenient for you.

I am sending under separate cover all of the background material which we have gathered. The state library was very helpful, and several of us did some independent research which also helped. If you have any questions regarding the material, I would appreciate it if you would let me know so I could get some information for you ahead of time.

Thanks again for your help. I'll call you shortly to set up an official appointment.

Sincerely,

Ruth Poe, Director
Elksburg Public Library

Before a formal meeting, be sure to send a decision maker relevant background information.

At a more formal meeting such as this, the librarian and trustee team should arrive promptly and be concise in their presentation or discussion. An elected official usually has very little time and is frustrated by the "long-winders"—those who talk and talk without getting to the point. If the meeting goes well, the librarian can be assured of additional meetings if necessary. If the meeting is a waste of time for the decision maker, the librarian may have a harder time getting an appointment next time. The librarian and trustee should prepare well, do their homework, and make their presentation informative and short. Ask the elected official for a certain time commitment and then stick to it. When the issue is complicated, request a longer meeting initially. Leave earlier rather than later. Do not stay after the time is up unless specifically asked to do so by the decision maker. This may all sound elementary, but many individuals take advantage of an audience with an elected official and decide to share everything they ever wanted to discuss with that person during one meeting in case they never get another chance. That approach may eliminate the opportunity for another chance!

Meeting at the Library

The librarian and trustee must also invite the elected official to the library to discuss library issues on their own turf. The setting makes a difference. Seeing a problem is more memorable than hearing about one. The types of meetings can vary. First, the library staff and trustees can invite the funding body to visit the library and follow a prepared agenda. Issue all guests a library card if they do not already have one. The librarian can give the officials a tour of

September 22, 1991

The Honorable John Vinich
P. O. Box 248
Elksburg, WY 82070

PUBLIC LIBRARY

Dear John:

I want to let you know again how helpful our meeting was last month. I am very excited about the prospects for the library district legislation. Without your help, I don't know where we would be by now. Thank you so much for offering to sponsor the bill for us. The library community across the state is thrilled to have you sponsor it. We would appreciate your thoughts on any co-sponsors you think would be helpful.

The trustees have their regular monthly board meeting next Tuesday at 4 p.m. I would appreciate it if you would be willing to talk with them for about ten minutes about the library district bill. William and I are now "up" on the particulars, and the rest of the board generally understands the problem, but any additional input you might have would be invaluable.

If you have time, we would like to have you take a tour of the library so you can see first-hand some of the problems we've discussed and how additional funding through a library district would resolves them. We will not keep you any longer than an hour. Thank you very much. I'll be in touch shortly.

Sincerely,

Ruth Poe, Director
Elksburg Public Library

An invitation to visit the library should include
a brief description of the agenda.

the facilities and conclude with a more formal information session, either with the whole group or individually. Inviting one governing official at a time takes more time but may be more effective because the entire staff can devote their attention to that person. On the other hand, sometimes questions by one official will "break the ice" or start another one thinking in a certain way. If the official is being toured alone, he or she may not want to reveal his or her ignorance by asking a "dumb" question.

October 8, 1991

The Honorable John Vinich
P. O. Box 248
Elksburg, WY 82070

PUBLIC LIBRARY

Dear John:

As I wrote you a couple of days ago, our board was very appreciative of the time you spent with us at the last library board meeting. The board members are now comfortable with how the bill has been drafted and confident that under your stewardship, the library district bill has a good chance of passing. I want to let you know that they understand that because district bills like this are often considered "tax increases" by other legislators that it could be difficult to get through. However, we all appreciate your efforts in helping us try.

The real reason I write, however, is to ask if you would be willing to serve as the "Award Distributor" at our annual Christmas Ball. As you know, between 300 and 400 individuals attend this event, and over the years it has become an evening that everyone looks forward to. Your "duties" at the dinner would include handing out plaques and certificates to the dance and costume winners as well as pulling door prize numbers. Your presence would certainly add an air of sophistication that we usually do not have! Thanks for considering it, and I hope you will join us.

I hope that your little girl is feeling better now. Those early fall colds can certainly hit hard.

Thanks again. I'll talk with you shortly.

Sincerely,

Ruth Poe, Director
Elksburg Public Library

Many decision makers are pleased to participate
in a special event at a library.

The library can also ask a governing official to participate in a planned event by the library. Officials are pleased to do so, especially if it is a highly visible program,[5] such as distributing summer reading program awards, recognizing volunteers at a volunteer tea, digging the first shovel of dirt at a ground-breaking ceremony, etc. Ask the press to attend, and make sure the official's name is printed on all public relations materials and press releases. Even if a decision maker is not part of the program, if he or she attends any library meeting or event, be sure to introduce him or her to the audience. Elected officials like to be associated with positive issues and causes, and very few voters dislike libraries. If a library event is not controversial, elected officials are usually delighted to attend or participate.

The librarian should also send invitations and agendas to the members of the library's governing body for all board meetings, receptions, and activities that are planned for the public.

October 21, 1991

Senator John Vinich
P. O. Box 248
Elksburg, WY 82070

PUBLIC LIBRARY

Dear John:

    The quarterly meeting of the Elk County Library Association is meeting in Elksburg on November 17 and 18. Over 54 librarians and staff from the region have already registered. I enclose a copy of the agenda and registration form for your information. As you see, we have marked the registration form "complimentary" so that if you decide to join us for any of the workshops or the meals, you will not have to pay for them.

    I know this is a busy time of year, but if you have the opportunity to stop by, everyone would love to meet you. You might also find some of the programs helpful for background information on the library district bill.

    Thanks for your continued support of libraries!

Sincerely,

Ruth Poe, Director
Elksburg Public Library

Inviting decision makers to your own convention is effective.

November 3, 1992

Senator John Vinich
P. O. Box 248
Elksburg, WY 82070

PUBLIC LIBRARY

Dear Senator Vinich:

    You are cordially invited to a continental breakfast sponsored by the Elksburg Public Library for the members of the Legislative Education Committee who will be holding an interim committee meeting in Elksburg on Nov. 25.

    The breakfast will be held from 7:30 a.m. to 9:00 a.m. in the meeting room of the Elksburg Public Library at 514 South 12th. No formal program is planned. You are welcome to stop by for a homemade roll, a glass of freshly squeezed orange juice and a gourmet cup of coffee before your 9:00 a.m. meeting.

    We appreciate it when the legislature meets in cities outside the capitol and are excited about your being here.

    Please r.s.v.p. by Nov. 20. We look forward to meeting you!

Sincerely,

William Findlay Schmich, Chair
Elksburg Public Library
Board of Trustees

P. S. John--As you know, we sent this letter to all members of your committee. We will be calling each of them before the breakfast even if we don't hear from them. Thanks for letting us know ahead of time that you were meeting here.

Capitalizing on events that bring legislators to town is very effective!

    A librarian may also organize a meeting specifically for the benefit of the decision makers dealing with library issues. At such a meeting, library representatives can present the library's budget or its plans for a potential building program, or they can speak about a peripheral issue that greatly affects it, such as a local tax initiative. Even if the officials cannot attend the meetings or programs, they will be aware of the library's activities as a result of the invitations.

Making a Presentation
to the Decision Makers

Librarians and trustees will often be asked by decision makers to make a formal budget request or presentation. Budget presentations are the most common type, although librarians may also be asked to explain the need for a building campaign, a fund-raising project, a new service, or other issues of importance to the library and to the community.

When making a presentation, a librarian should be well-prepared and stay within the allotted time. Elected officials, like students, stop listening when a presentation drags on beyond the time it is supposed to end. Make a thorough presentation, but if time is running short, let the decision makers know you know your time is up and let them decide whether you should receive extra time or not.

If more than one person from the library is making a presentation, the amount of time each person gets (and takes) should be calculated precisely and kept on target. Problems with multiple presenters occur when a decision maker has a question for a presenter during that person's time allotment. The person should always answer the question politely and in as much detail as necessary. In order to anticipate the additional time necessary for unsolicited questions, the librarian coordinating the presentation needs either to add a couple of minutes for questions on to each person's time or to allow time for questions at the end and be flexible if the entire time allotted is used up prior to the question/answer period.

If the time is running out and the presentations are not completed because the governing body asked so many questions, the librarian or trustee in charge should point out to the decision makers that the library's time allotment is almost over but that the presenters still have additional input for the board. The librarian should then give the board the options of extending the presentation, scheduling an additional presentation, or requesting that the library submit the additional testimony in writing. The latter is the least effective, because the library will not have the opportunity to reinforce the written testimony orally or answer questions the decision makers might have. Decision makers will be pleased the library is concerned about not going over its time allotment in any case.

When the library makes a presentation to a state legislative committee, the process is called *testifying* even though the presenters are not sworn in or interrogated by lawyers. The time concerns mentioned above also apply to testifying before legislative bodies. One additional word of caution is required here, however. Librarians should be prepared to wait for long periods of time before they are called to testify. To some extent, local governing bodies adhere to a more rigid timetable than do legislative committees. Often a legislative committee will run hours or even a day or more behind schedule. Librarians must be patient as they wait for their turn, however frustrating that might be. A good example of a frustrating situation was relayed to me by a head of a department in another state. The legislative budget committee asked him to appear before them regarding their budget. He lived outside the capital, so he flew in the night before in order to make his morning presentation. He sat in the committee all morning long, not able to leave in case they called him. He sat there all afternoon as well, as the committee discussed budgets with other agencies. As it became later and later, the audience cleared out, and the legislators also began leaving one by one because of other commitments. Finally, only the committee chair and the department head were in the room. The legislator indicated it was now the department head's turn and asked, "Have you changed any of the figures that you originally sent us?" When the department head answered in the negative, the legislator continued, "Well, that's all I have." It was too late to fly back, so the department head spent another night at the capital. It took three days of the department head's time to answer a simple "no" to one question! One must hope this kind of situation does not happen very often, because it is a waste of taxpayers' money and the library's time. Librarians need to be aware that situations like this do occur, however, and to be prepared for them.

A presentation to decision makers should be lively, and a librarian or trustee should use props, pictures, graphics, or other visual aids when possible. As mentioned previously, many people learn better by seeing than by hearing. If your oral testimony is aided by written overhead transparencies, the decision makers are more likely to remember the content of your request, especially if the transparencies are done well. It is frustrating to look at an overhead transparency that consists of a copy of the material already distributed, or that consists solely of small typewritten paragraphs. Use imaginative, thoughtful transparencies that are easy to read and understand.

Supportive written documentation should be sent well ahead of time so that the officials theoretically have plenty of time to review it. Remember, even though the officials received these materials, they may not have had the time to read them. You can expect at least two of the decision makers to ask the same question during the same meeting. It is hard to both think and listen sometimes, and, since this is what officials are required to do, they miss a lot of information.

Part of the objective of a presentation is to give the governing body the message you want to get across at least six times in a very short span of time. (See page 43 on insurance sales!) A good way to do this is to start by sending decision makers your information in a detailed document and providing them with a short summary (two times). Then state the important points at least two times in an oral presentation, and present the point again in written form on a board or in some kind of a visual aid at least once during the oral presentation (five times). Finally, in a follow-up thank-you letter, include the main point at least once. The rule of six can be followed in any kind of situation in which you want someone to remember your main points!

If a librarian or trustee is testifying to a governing body regarding a specific topic not necessarily related to the library, the same rules should apply. However, usually the main group affected will be making the primary presentation, and the library is providing additional testimony. It is important to contact the main presenter before the meeting so that the groups can coordinate efforts. Although repetition is good, redundancy is not.

Other General Recommendations

Planning an Attack

Librarians are well-known for their creativity, their resourcefulness, and their cooking abilities. All three of these attributes come in handy when implementing a lobbying effort.

As with any kind of campaign, the first thing is to know what you want. The library director and trustees must have a goal clearly in mind before they embark on a lobbying effort. Decision makers always want to know the "bottom line"—what you want and how much it will cost. Although it is easy to want a big budget, it is not as easy for librarians and trustees to agree upon priorities within that budget. Once they reach a consensus, the library director and trustees still have to articulate their needs on paper and agree that it reflects what they agreed on! As mentioned elsewhere in this book, the library must speak with one voice and tell one story to be most effective. Although this is time-consuming, it is worth the effort.

The next step is to prepare a big calendar. Start with the target date of the goal for which the library needs to lobby and work backward. Suppose, for example, that the library wants to obtain an increased budget. The budget hearings are May 28, and the current date is November 3. On the big calendar square for May 28, mark with a pencil or erasable marker, "Budget Hearing." On May 27, mark, "Reminder calls to friend testimonials." On May 21, write, "Send final copy budget and summary to county supervisors." Continue to use your imagination to try to fill in as much detail as possible, in reverse order, in preparing for the budget hearing. Include everything imaginable as a starter. The calendar items will change in time; some activities will be added, some deleted. At least the calendar will organize your thoughts and efforts in the right direction.

Developing Personal Relationships

In addition to working on a specific goal as outlined in yourcalendar, the library should develop a simultaneous program to increase elected officials' awareness of the library and to get to know those decision makers personally. A study of how much library directors and trustees interacted with elected officials and how much elected officials actually used the library showed that the library's representatives in this case were not "deeply involved" with their governing body.[6] The librarians and trustees did not belong to the same social or fraternal organizations as the municipal administrator or council members. Neither the library trustees nor the library director attended municipal council meetings. The council members did not attend the library meetings and did not, for the most part, receive minutes from those meetings. Only six of the twenty-five council members used the library on a regular basis. As the author of the article asks, can a library "afford this splendid isolation as it competes for today's scarce public funds?"[7] Another study showed that libraries with librarians who extensively interacted with municipal officials and had active public relations programs received greater local tax support.[8] One can conclude that an effort to increase interaction with elected officials is legitimate and will most likely increase the library's overall standing with the decision makers.

Negative Lobbying

The library lobbyist always needs to be upbeat. Showing anger, however justifiable, is usually ineffective. Being impatient with ignorant legislators is harmful even though it may feel good at the time. Remember that most decision makers are ignorant (that is, without knowledge) in many areas because they must deal with so many issues. Your input is therefore extremely important to the ignorant legislator. Instead of focusing on legislators who do not support your efforts in an attempt to "expose them to the public," make a big public fuss about those who support you.

Many believe that negative campaigns work and point to dirty tactics used in national campaigns to prove they are effective. The librarian has to be careful if contemplating such an action. For example, in Wyoming a special interest group went after twelve legislators for not voting in a certain way and called them "The Dirty Dozen." They took out big negative newspaper ads in the legislators' hometowns, issued press releases, and aired many negative radio spots against the twelve. In spite of all the bad publicity, all of them were reelected. The marked legislators were proud of the label and got buttons showing who they were. The campaign changed few minds about the legislators, but it did have other effects. It destroyed the credibility of the group that came up with the plan, and it angered other legislators who felt the label was unfair. Librarians should think twice before embarking on a negative campaign. They should take into consideration the general attitude of the citizens in the town, city, county, district, or state. A negative campaign might work in some areas, but it could backfire and end in disaster in others.

Notes

1. Kathleen Kelly Rummel and Esther Perica, *Persuasive Public Relations for Libraries* (Chicago: American Library Association, 1983); Steve Shurman, *ABC's of Library Promotion*, 2nd ed. (Metuchen, N.J.: Scarecrow, 1980).

2. Herbert S. White, Dean of the Library School at Indiana at the time this article was published, has this to say about politicians: "They will only use us for their own purposes and we will inherit their enemies . . . " and "Ultimately politicians are pragmatists who do what earns them credit toward their next objective." "The Danger of Political Polarization for Librarianship," *Library Journal* 114 (15 June 1989): 40–41.

3. Georgia Robertson, ed., *Nebraska Trustee Handbook* (Lincoln: The Nebraska Library Commission and The Trustees, Users and Friends Section of the Nebraska Library Association, 1990), 123.

4. Ibid.

5. Ibid.

6. Virgil L. P. Blake, "Library and Municipal Officials: The Great Divide," *The Bottom Line* 3, no. 2 (1989): 30–31, reprinted in *The Leadership Role of Library Trustees: 4th Annual Trustee Institute* (Harrisburg: State Library of Pennsylvania, Pennsylvania Library Association Trustee Division, May 11 and 12, 1990).

7. Ibid.

8. Ibid., 31, quoting Patricia Berger, "An Investigation of the Relationship Between Public Relations Activities and Budget Allocation in Public Libraries," *Information Processing and Management* 15 (November 1979): 179–193.

Lobbying State Legislatures

This chapter deals with general information about approaching state legislatures, much of which will be applicable to any state. Lobbying state legislatures requires a good understanding of the legislative process. Librarians therefore need to get to know the power structure and inner workings of their own state legislature in order to be successful in this arena.

Librarians must also recognize that the issues at the state level are different from those at the local level. Librarians lobby local officials or administrators primarily for the majority of their operating budget. Public librarians must also persuade the appropriate local governing body to place tax referenda on the ballot, to issue bonds, to approve zoning changes or exceptions, and the like. In contrast, librarians turn to state legislators for enabling legislation for library districts, allowing localities to fund libraries or to obtain more funding (usually tax initiatives) that might impact their library, and for other kinds of legislation, such as patron record privacy.

State and local constituencies also differ. Local decision makers are accountable solely to the people in their voting district, and they often represent the library's "court of last resort." If they reject the library's issue, the librarian may not have an alternative governing body to approach. Although a state-elected official's primary constituents are the people in his or her district, the state legislator also represents all other citizens in the state. Therefore, librarians should feel comfortable contacting any or all legislators about an issue of statewide importance, keeping in mind that legislators will usually be most responsive to the librarians in their own district. Even so, the legislators may not vote the way their local librarians want them to vote, especially if the library issue involves funding and the state coffers are limited. Librarians can then turn to more supportive state legislators in other districts.

Profile of a Typical Legislator

Many states do not have professional legislatures, that is, legislatures that meet full time or the equivalent of full time. Instead, these states have part-time or "citizen" legislatures made up of legislators who usually have other full-time jobs in addition to their legislative duties. Both full- and part-time legislators sit on one or more committees dealing with specific issues, such as education, agriculture, health, labor, business, etc. The committees meet while the legislatures are in session and during the *interim* (the period between sessions when the legislatures are part-time) to consider bills dealing with their subject areas. Librarians should determine what kind of legislature their state has, because it can make a difference regarding what kind of a person to expect in the position of legislator.

A full-time legislator will usually have an office with staff and aides. In addition to spending time in session or committee meetings, a full-time legislator will devote his or her attention and efforts to becoming knowledgeable about the issues facing the legislature and the problems facing the state. The number of issues is so great that even a full-time legislator cannot be an expert in everything. Consequently, aides will research the issues and brief the legislators about them. The librarian-lobbyist needs to determine who is responsible for library issues and get to know these people well.

A part-time legislator may or may not have an office at the capitol building or elsewhere, and may or may not have staff or aides to help with research. Often, the time spent debating bills in session at the capitol is limited. When part-time legislators are not in session, they are making a living at other jobs in their home districts.

They may pay a lot of attention to issues during the session and when preparing for committee meetings, but they will generally know fewer details about issues facing the state than their full-time counterparts in other states. They face the impossible task of taking a stand on state issues without staff support and often without sufficient information to make an informed decision. One part-time legislator remarked that when he was first elected, he could hardly wait to get to the capital so he could learn everything, and when he got there, they all expected him to know it already.

Part-time legislators are mostly concerned, well-meaning people with charisma and a keen ability to communicate with large groups of people. They are aware of general problems and general solutions to those problems. They may be experts in the areas covered in the committees on which they sit. When voting, they often trust other legislators to help them on issues with which they are not familiar. They do not have a lot of time to study a specific issue unless it is a committee topic. Of course, there are exceptions to these general statements, and over the years, part-time legislators who stay in office for a long time become relatively familiar with and have a good understanding of most of the issues.

If a librarian-lobbyist considers how much he or she knows about the library profession, how long it took to learn it, and how much there is to know about it, he or she can easily understand that even a good legislator, especially the part-timers, will have only a superficial understanding of the library profession and its problems. Often what a legislator will say in debate or committee on behalf of a library bill is exactly what you give them to say. Legislators are good at performing, at embellishing, and at repeating information. Do not expect them to go much beyond that. Again, exceptions exist, but the average legislator simply does not have the time, the energy, or the capacity to know what you know and what every other individual involved in a special interest knows.

Consequently, as this book will state many times, the library lobbyist needs to treat legislators as if they are totally ignorant every time the librarian makes a presentation to them. This does not mean treating them as though they are stupid—just ignorant of the facts. In fact, as recommended in Chapter 6, avoid being arrogant or condescending to legislators. It is difficult to treat individuals as if they are ignorant and not be condescending at the same time, but it is something a good lobbyist needs to learn how to do. Librarians must explain simply the issue, the potential resolutions, and the action wanted from the legislators, and then they must repeat it often. Simplicity and repetition are key words when dealing with legislators.

The higher the level of governance, the greater the number (and perhaps the complexity) of issues. Remember this and treat your legislators kindly and with patience. They will appreciate it, and the library will benefit as a result.

Legislative Budget Concerns

The number of library-related funding issues facing state legislatures is phenomenal. A quick perusal of the 1990 ALA *Yearbook of Facts* shows many legislative requests by states in just one year. Connecticut requested funding for bonds, public library construction, and the state's Cooperating Library Service Units to name a few items.[1] Florida asked for additional funding for state aid to public libraries.[2] The Indiana State Library was reviewed by the Sunset Committee of the Indiana General Assembly, which recommended, among other things, automating Indiana libraries.[3] In Maine, the state library along with three other cultural agencies—the State Museum, the Arts Commission, and the Historic Preservation Commission—proposed a Maine Community Cultural Alliance to seek new and increased funding for the agencies and their allied community-based organizations.[4] The New Hampshire legislature passed legislation making library records confidential, effective in 1989.[5]

As this sample shows, although states do not provide the major part of most libraries' operating budgets, state legislatures address many library fiscal issues; even more such issues will appear as the economic outlook changes and as new technologies bring libraries closer together.

Library lobbyists may not need to lobby annually for legislation involving budgetary matters or funding for other programs. Some states have biennial budgets, and some state statutes governing issues such as state aid may be perpetual unless there is a sunset date or an automatic audit cycle. As a result, the library lobbyist must know what statutes need to be reauthorized when and then carefully plan a strategy to work with other librarians across the state to coordinate lobbying efforts. Statewide legislation cannot usually be passed through the efforts of one library alone. Librarians must cooperate and coordinate their lobbying efforts as they attempt to pass funding legislation for libraries.

Public Libraries

Public libraries receive a majority of their funding from local sources.[6] Issues related to the operating budgets of public libraries are rarely of concern to state legislators, except as they relate to one another and to national averages. For example, legislators may be concerned if counties or cities in one part of the state spend $55.00 per capita on libraries because they are located in an area which is rich in local taxes, while counties or cities in another part of the state spend only $3.55 per capita because their tax base is minimal. Public librarians usually lobby the state legislature for direct state aid to public libraries, for categorical funding, or for additional funding for the state library to distribute to local libraries through grants or services. Often legislatures will fund library aid programs to correct such inequities as in the example above or to bring state spending on libraries up to a level comparable with other states.

School, Academic, and State Libraries

School libraries receive a greater percentage of their funding from the state than do public libraries because they are part of state-funded public education. Although the state may have responsibility for the direct funding of school libraries, the actual dollar amounts appropriated to a school media center are more a matter of local discretion.

The budget of a state-funded college or university library may be scrutinized by the legislature directly or as part of the greater university budget, depending on the funding scheme for universities and colleges within the state.

The state library is a branch of state government and is directly funded by the state legislature.

Planning a Lobbying Effort

Laying the Foundation

Because one library cannot usually pass legislation alone, a librarian who is interested in passing such legislation must work through the state library association or with a small group of libraries if only a few are affected. The first step is to contact the appropriate library supporters in the state to see if they are interested in the legislation. Additional information on coordinating with other librarians around the state will be discussed later in this chapter.

The next important step is to begin preparing information files on each legislator in your district. A good librarian-lobbyist needs to have as much information, personal and political, about a legislator as possible. A librarian can gather this information from newspaper articles, *Who's Who* publications, discussions with people who know the legislator, publications distributed by the statewide taxpayer's association or by the state (check at the state capitol building for availability), and from personal interaction.

After every interaction, take the time to write down everything you remember that you might want to use again. This information can include such things as the legislator's sick pet, a family vacation, favorite desserts or books, accomplishments about which the legislator is proud, and so on. It never hurts to personalize a letter to a legislator, even if the body of the letter is the same you write to everyone else. Start a letter (or a conversation) with, "How did that visit from your mother go?" or "Did your kids finally get over the chicken pox?" or "We just got the latest novel by your favorite author. Would you like to check it out?" They will be amazed and delighted you remembered something about them, and even a form letter will seem personal. Review this file each time before you interact with a legislator, and make sure that it is up-to-date so you do not ask about a dead parent or a divorced spouse.

The Key Players

STATE LIBRARY ASSOCIATION

The state library association will often play a major part in lobbying at the state level. It most likely will hire a lobbyist to help the statewide effort and have a legislative committee in place that is already politically involved on an ongoing basis. The members of the association may also adopt a platform or pass a resolution in support of or against a particular bill.[7]

The state library association may pass a resolution for or against a bill, especially if the statewide library community is united in its views.

Platform statements or resolutions should be scrutinized by members of the association before the vote. If the association is split in its support of the legislation, it should evaluate carefully whether or not to recommend the legislation for action. It does

ELK COUNTY
LIBRARY ASSOCIATION
RESOLUTION

PUBLIC LIBRARY

Whereas, libraries in the state are underfunded
and possible sources for funding are limited, and

Whereas, counties in the state have widely
differing tax bases because of the disparity
in natural resources and because of the tax
exemption on property owned by government, and

Whereas, library services in counties without a
strong tax base will have to be curtailed
drastically unless a new source of funding becomes
available to them, and

Whereas, the citizens of the state have repeatedly
demonstrated their support of libraries through
maximum local funding efforts, tapping all
sources currently available to them through the
statutes, and

Whereas, creation of library districts would enable,
but not mandate, citizens to tax themselves
additionally for library services,

BE IT THEREFORE RESOLVED THAT:

the Elk County Library Association
consisting of thirty-eight member libraries
endorses Senate File 102, Library Districts,
sponsored by Senator John Vinich.

Eloise Lucile Kinney, President
Elk County Library Association
December 30, 1991

not look good for librarians in one district to fight librarians in another.

PROFESSIONAL LIBRARY LOBBYIST

As mentioned previously, many state library associations hire a part-time or full-time professional lobbyist. A detailed discussion of the pros and cons of hiring a professional lobbyist is found in another chapter. Sometimes a library association can share a lobbyist with one or more other not-for-profit organizations. The on-site professional lobbyist at the capital complements the at-home efforts of the public librarians, trustees, and library supporters. Professional lobbyists have the time and the expertise to follow legislation at the state level closely.[8] Votes and amendments occur so fast that if someone is not constantly watchdogging the bill and contacting the appropriate forces at home, librarians can make major mistakes or suffer major losses.

THE HOME-DISTRICT SUPPORTERS

When the librarian-lobbyist organizes supporters to contact their legislators, a wide variety of individuals representing different interests should be included as part of the lobbying team. Legislators are impressed when individuals outside the anticipated group of supporters contact them. For instance, one year I received more than 400 letters from a small community regarding education funding. The writers identified themselves as bankers, lawyers, doctors, gasoline station attendants, etc.

January 2, 1992

The Honorable John Vinich
Senate Chambers
State Capitol Building
Cheyenne, WY 82002

PUBLIC LIBRARY

Dear Senator Vinich:

I understand that you are sponsoring a bill to create library districts in the state. I would like to lend my support to your effort and am sending a similar letter to all of the senators on the education committee and from my county. You are welcome to use my letter in any way if you think it might help.

Public libraries represent the best of the "American way of life." While our values nationwide seem to be lost in rampant crime, broken families, unemployment and bad economic times, the public library still stands as a tribute to what is right with our society. They provide an escape for those who are burdened with troubles; they provide pleasure for those without money; and they provide education for those who want to better themselves. Anything we can do to continue their viability is important to the well-being of our society.

As you know, our property taxes differ so widely in the state that some counties have few dollars available to fund libraries, while others have sufficient funding for all of their services, including libraries. I support your efforts to pass legislation authorizing optional library districts which would allow the poorer counties to levy additional mills earmarked for libraries. If people want library services enough to tax themselves, please give them the means whereby they can do it.

Thank you for your support and your vote.

Sincerely,

Lisa Kinney
Attorney at Law
LK:rpl

"Uninvolved" library lobbyists can effectively write on your behalf.

It was a tremendously powerful effort that gained the attention of the education committee members and eventually resulted in at least a partial victory.[9]

THE LEGISLATORS THEMSELVES

Obviously, your legislators will play a big role in any effort you undertake to pass legislation. Bringing them in early helps ensure success, or at least advocacy. The more a legislator knows about an issue, the more able he or she will be to debate the accompanying legislation effectively. In addition, legislators often know the tricks of the trade in their own legislature and key people to contact.

In the event that a legislator or legislators cannot be on a steering committee or actively participate in meetings, librarians should nevertheless send them notices and minutes of the meetings. Then, if the legislators can attend, they will, and if they cannot, they may take the time to at least read what happened.

THE BUREAUCRATS

Next to legislators, bureaucrats are the most powerful individuals of whom librarian lobbyists should be aware when they attempt to pass library legislation. Statutes often authorize the state through its agencies to carry out or not carry out certain actions. The agencies then implement the statutes through "rules and regulations." These rules and regulations attempt to define in detail the legislative scheme behind the statute so that all persons enforcing the new law will work under specific and uniform guidelines. The people who write these rules and regulations are extremely powerful: they can take a simply worded statute and develop detailed rules that may or may not reflect accurately what the legislature intended.

Statutes are often written broadly. Individuals writing rules and regulations try to determine the *legislative intent* before they write the implementing rules and regulations. Legislative intent is determined by recorded debate, history of amendments, committee reports, committee minutes, and so on. In some states it is extremely difficult to determine what the legislature's intent was because no official documentation exists. Even if someone can point to newspaper articles or committee votes to bolster an argument about how the legislature thought a law would be implemented, without official methods of recordation, these sources are insufficient.

If the legislative intent is unclear or hard to determine, the rule makers have to develop rules that reflect what they think the legislature wanted to accomplish or what they believe is workable. You might even say that they rewrite the law after the law is passed! Usually the governor, a committee of legislators, sponsoring legislators or committees, or others must approve the accompanying rules to make sure that the rules accurately reflect legislative intent. The group approving the rules may like the bureaucrats' interpretation of the statute or it may fail to pay close attention to the rules. If no one challenges the rules, the bureaucrats will essentially be able to write a law that may differ from the true legislative intent.

A simple example of the rule makers' power can be shown by examining a theoretical library aid bill. Suppose the legislature passed a bill for state aid to public libraries that stated, "Every public library serving a population of up to 25,000 individuals will receive X dollars. Every public library serving a population between

25,000 and 100,000 will receive Y dollars. Every public library serving populations of over 100,000 will receive Z dollars." Certainly the intent is clear, and the implementing body will be able to dole out the cash easily. Right? Perhaps not. First, what about a branch library? Do branch libraries in different cities each get additional funds? What about the population served? What if the public library is in a city which is across the river from another city without a public library? Even though on paper the population served is the city of A, the public library really has about double the number of users because the citizens of city B use the library, too. Do they get extra money? What about a town of 100 without a library? Could it set one up in someone's house or off city hall and then get state aid for it? The individuals who write rules and regulations have to anticipate the details that the statute does not address and determine how to handle each of the above situations (plus more!) based on the ephemeral legislative intent. Where there is none, the bureaucrats use their best judgment. For this reason the librarian-lobbyist must get to know these individuals if possible.

The rule makers usually work in the capital city, so it is hard for most librarians to get to know them, or even to know who they are. Librarians on the legislative committee or librarians in the capital city need to find out who will write the rules for the library legislation. They then need to discuss the legislation with the bureaucrats if possible and offer to help them understand the needs of the libraries and the reasons behind the original legislation.

If it is impossible to get to know the bureaucrats, the librarian-lobbyist can affect the rules and regulations in other ways. Often, public hearings will be held on proposed rules and regulations, and librarians can testify. The law in many states provides mechanisms to require the state to hold hearings under certain circumstances. Librarians should review the proposed rules and regulations and if they disagree with them, and no public hearings are scheduled, librarians should trigger the legal mechanism for public hearings if possible. The alert librarian-lobbyist needs to know that when the statute passes both houses and the governor signs a bill, it is not necessarily time to relax!

The First Effort

As previously mentioned, after preparing good information on each legislator and determining your legislative goals, it is time to approach the legislators to introduce yourself if you do not yet know them. Although legislators cannot spend a great deal of time with each constituent, they like to have regular contact with constituents and most likely will be glad to meet with you. Once you feel comfortable with your legislators, you can begin developing a strategy to pass (or kill) the legislation you want.

The Legislation

Creating Bills

Legislation can be developed in several ways. A bill is often created after a concerned citizen contacts a legislator with a problem. After discussing the problem with the constituent, a legislator will contact the legislative drafting office in the state and ask the office to draft a bill under the legislator's sponsorship. When the legislator receives the first draft from the office, he or she will verify its contents with the constituent. After appropriate changes are made, the legislator returns the bill to the office for final processing.

Instead of relying on verbal discussions for the initial draft, librarians and others can take preliminary steps that might save time and clarify their legislative needs before approaching a legislator. A librarian or library committee can prepare a rough draft of a bill themselves or compile elements of what they want included in a piece of legislation and give it to a sponsor. The sponsor discusses the draft or elements with them and then gives it to the legislative drafting office to rewrite it to conform with the state's statutes. Librarians can hire an attorney to draft even a closer facsimile of the version of a bill they want to give to the sponsor. The sponsor must still give it to the legislative drafting office, but the final bill will probably be close to the version written by the attorney. Finally, librarians may find a statute that they like from another state, modify it to their needs, and give it to the sponsor. Again, the bill will go through a legislative drafting office to conform it to the state's format.

Librarians must make sure the legislation is written carefully and accomplishes what the librarians want it to accomplish. Too often, a bill is represented to the members of the house or senate as accomplishing what the sponsors want and so the bill is passed. Legislators find out later that the wording was insufficient or the law was placed in the wrong part of the statutes, and therefore the

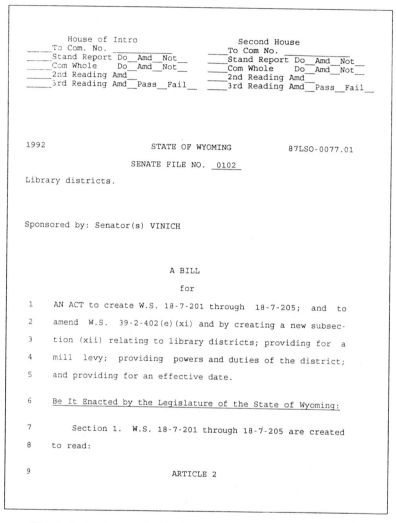

This is the first page of a bill that conforms to Wyoming's format.

law is void or inoperable. Some states keep a sufficient record of legislative intent to save a bill that needs interpretation. As mentioned previously, legislative intent is shown through recorded floor debate, committee reports, inserts into a daily log, and other recorded evidence of the goals a legislature collectively agreed upon when it passed a particular bill. In other states, such as Wyoming, no

records of legislative intent exist, so interpretation of all legislation is based on the words of the statutes themselves. Librarians in
those states must therefore carefully scrutinize the proposed statutory wording.

The creators of the bill may not necessarily be the individuals
who do a major share of the lobbying. Although a small group of
librarians may take the initiative to create a bill, a paid lobbyist or a
legislative committee of the state association is often responsible for
"shepherding" the bill through the process. A bill usually does not
pass without a cast of thousands, however. A network of supportive
librarians, trustees, citizens, and local decision makers must also
become familiar with the bill after it is in final form. They will be
called upon to contact legislators at the appropriate time, and they
usually make the difference between a successful lobbying effort
and an unsuccessful one.[10]

Bill Sponsors

A bill should have as many sponsors as is possible and politically
feasible. A legislator sponsors a bill when he or she agrees to have
his or her name listed as a sponsor. A *primary sponsor* is the legislator whose name appears first on the bill and who is a member
of the house where the bill originates. The primary sponsor often
presents the bill to the appropriate standing committee and to the
committee of the whole (all legislators sitting as one big committee)
when it is first debated. Other cosponsors are listed behind the primary sponsor and play a secondary support role. If the members
of more than half of both houses are official sponsors of a bill, it
is practically guaranteed a successful journey through the political
process. Such overwhelming outward support of a bill usually does
not exist, unfortunately. Instead, the bill will have a varying number of sponsors, depending on the bill, how the legislators were
approached, and the rules of the legislature.

The primary sponsors and cosponsors should be picked politically and practically. When searching for a primary sponsor, try
to find someone who believes the library's need is appealing and
who supports the legislation heartily.[11] He or she will speak for it
with conviction. Legislators are usually interested in what can be
done for constituents at home and how their sponsorship of and
comments about a certain bill look to their constituents. Successfully sponsoring a bill beneficial to libraries is politically beneficial
to the sponsors.

Also try to find the right blend of primary sponsors or cosponsors. For example, even though I am in the minority party, because of my background in libraries, I am a very good and credible sponsor of any library legislation. However, I also recommend to the proponents of any library legislation that I cosponsor it with a senator from the other political party and with one legislator from each party in the house. A balanced party- and house-sponsorship helps make the bill more credible as well.

If the speaker of the house, president of the senate, or powerful committee heads are willing to cosponsor the bill, their names on the bill will usually guarantee that it moves smoothly through the proper channels. The other sponsoring legislators can do the legwork and prepare the background information. Cosponsorship gives the bill the benefit of the prestigious names while not burdening the leaders with additional work.

Compromise Position

The sponsors of a bill may want to agree beforehand on what kinds of compromises, if any, they are willing to make. As a bill works its way through the legislative process, it can undergo many changes. At some point, if the changes are too great, the library community may want to say, "Call it off if possible!" More often, the library community must compromise and say, "We don't like the changes, but we can live with them because the rest of the bill is important."

It is impossible to anticipate prior to submitting the legislation to the legislature every possible change that might be made to it. Librarians should try to control the changes by having backup recommendations ready to offer if the legislators do not like the legislation or parts of it as written. If the changes are left to the imagination of the legislators, the librarians may find themselves with a law that does the opposite of what they want.

The Legislative Process

How Bills Become Law

No two state legislatures operate in an identical fashion, but a majority of legislatures follow the general pattern of how a bill becomes law.[12]

Table 3   How a Bill Typically Becomes Law at the State Level

Introducing a Bill—An Overview

As shown above, the process of introducing a bill is as follows. Once the sponsor signs a bill indicating his or her acceptance of its final form, the bill is given to the presiding officer who is usually the president of the senate or house or the assembly speaker. This person assigns the bill to a committee. The committee chair schedules a public hearing on the bill or places the bill on an agenda for a committee hearing. After the committee discusses the bill, they vote it up or down, with or without amendments. In some states, bills can only be amended in committee. Librarian-lobbyists need to know if that is the procedure in their state. Sometimes a committee chair will not schedule a bill for hearing and, in effect, "pocket vetoes" it.

If the bill is given a positive recommendation from the committee, it is voted "out" of committee. The bill usually returns to the house of origin for presentation by the sponsor to the committee of the whole. The house debates the bill and then votes on it. The votes usually take place on different days and are called *committee-of-the-whole debate, second reading,* and *third reading.* Rules (discussed below) usually allow legislatures to expedite the process so that more than one reading and vote can occur on one day if necessary.

If the bill survives the three votes and is voted on favorably by one house, the same process is followed in the other house. If the bill gets through two houses without changes, it goes to the governor to sign. If one of the houses makes changes the other dislikes, the bill goes to a conference committee, where representatives from both houses discuss the changes and decide which amendments from each house will be kept. The conference committee members report the agreed-upon changes to their respective bodies and ask for approval. If they get it, the bill usually goes to the governor to sign. If the houses do not adopt the conference committee report, the bill is assigned to another conference committee composed of the same members or new ones. A conference committee can be closed or open. If it is closed, the committee can compromise only between the house position and the senate position. If it is an open conference committee, the members can rewrite the bill from scratch if they want. Conference committees are therefore very powerful. Library lobbyists need to attend these conference committee meetings and be prepared to provide testimony or documentation quickly, although often additional testimony is not taken.

After both houses adopt the conference committee recommendations, the bill goes to the governor. When the governor signs it, it will become law at the stated date in the bill. If the governor vetoes the bill while the legislature is still in session, the legislature may try to override the veto.

Rules of Order

Although the general flow of bills does not differ greatly from legislature to legislature, the procedures used can be quite different. Most legislatures adopt rules of order. In many states, each house adopts its own rules, which may differ from those of the other house.[13] The rules they follow are very important and the librarian-lobbyist must be very familiar with these rules in order to keep any proposed library legislation on track. Often, the person or persons knowing and understanding the rules best have the most power. Certainly, knowledge of the rules is key to ensuring smooth passage of the bill through the system.

Legislative Committees

Legislative committees do the "homework" for the legislature during the interim and spend a great deal of time meeting during the session to vote on bills.[14] They receive all the necessary background information to determine the merit of a bill. They listen to testimony from the agency or individuals involved or concerned about the legislation. They often hold public hearings during the interim between legislative sessions to obtain feedback from the general public. As a result, legislators not on a particular committee listen carefully to debate and comments by committee members when they present a bill. The committees are the experts in the area, and if a legislator has a question about a particular bill being introduced, he or she informally queries a member of the committee. When asked about a committee bill by other legislators, supportive committee members have the opportunity to do a little informal lobbying. They can say, "This is a good bill. Your constituency will really like it," or they can help calm any fears a reluctant legislator may have about a particular piece of legislation. The more sympathetic and united the committee, the better off the bill will be.

Committee Bill Assignments

A major first step in passing a piece of legislation is to get the bill assigned to a "friendly" committee, that is, a committee comprising legislators who have been lobbied and are in favor of the bill, or a committee knowledgeable about library issues and more likely to be sympathetic. For example, if a library bill is assigned to the Education Committee, it might have more support than if it were assigned to the Agriculture Committee. Often, if the legislative leader in charge of assignments gives a library bill to an unusual committee (such as the Agriculture Committee just mentioned), it may mean that the leader is against the legislation, and the bill is in trouble already. Some "killer" committees also exist, so that if a bill is assigned there, you know it is already doomed. In the past in Wyoming, a non-rule bill given to the Rules Committee was DOA.

In over three-quarters of the states, the presiding officer or another leader refers bills to committee.[15] If there is a question about where the bill should go, this person should be lobbied ahead of time to make sure the bill does not go to a committee that will hear it unfavorably or not hear it at all. Since most states do not have a committee dealing exclusively with library matters, some flexibility exists as to which committee will hear it. Librarians need to know some background on the members of each committee to which a library bill will likely be assigned and, if possible, know how each member intends to vote. Librarians in each home district must meet with their representatives before a session begins or before a library bill is introduced in order to educate the legislators about it.

It is easy to determine who is responsible in each legislature for assigning bills to committees. The librarians from the home district of that person should contact him or her before the session to set up a meeting as soon as the librarians know their bill will be introduced. One of the first questions the librarians need to ask at that meeting is which committee will be assigned the bill. If the legislator has not yet determined the committee assignment (and this will more often than not be the case if the question is asked early), the librarians should have a committee in mind to suggest to the legislator. If possible, try to get a commitment from the legislator to assign it to a certain committee.

The local librarians should check in with the assigner once the legislative session begins and before the bill is assigned to make sure nothing has changed in the legislator's decision to assign the bill to a certain committee, or to determine the committee assignment if no commitment had been made. Remember, if a bill is assigned to an unfriendly committee, it makes no difference that the majority of the rest of the legislature might have voted in favor of it if they had had an opportunity to do so. A bill must get out of a committee before the entire legislative body can hear it.

If the bill gets less than a majority vote in committee, it will die and progress no further in the legislative process, although there are ways, determined by the rules, to bring a bill back from the dead! If the bill gets more than 50 percent of the vote, it will pass out of committee and go on to the house of origin's *general file*, the list of bills for which a committee has voted favorably and sent to the body as a whole for a recommendation.

The Calendaring Process

The calendaring process is important because how the calendar is set and who controls it determine the priority of legislation for action. One philosophy is that the calendar must be strictly controlled by leadership so that important bills are not delayed by less critical measures. An opposite perspective holds that legislation should come up for debate in a fair and expeditious manner without regard to the preferences of one or two legislators.[16]

Generally, legislators use one of three methods to calendar bills for floor debate: (1) an automatic calendar that lists bills in the order reported from committee; (2) an order of business set by the presiding officer or some other leader; or (3) a schedule determined by a rules or calendaring committee. Some states use a combination of the above to give the leadership some discretion. For example, in the Alabama senate and the Mississippi house, the Rules Committee can "special order" a bill for consideration. In New Hampshire, bill are placed on the calendar in alphabetical order. In the Hawaii, Maryland, New Mexico, and Pennsylvania senates, the Secretary of the senate sets the calendar, while in the American Samoa, Massachusetts, and Vermont houses, the clerk sets it.[17] The individuals who control the calendar are the ones the librarian-lobbyist needs to get to know. Following is a list of states and how they determine their calendars.

Automatic or In Order Received

Alabama Senate and
  House
Arkansas House
California Senate and
  Assembly
Colorado Senate
Connecticut Senate
Delaware Senate
Georgia Senate
Idaho Senate and House
Kentucky Senate
Louisiana Senate and
  House
Maine House
Maryland House

Massachusetts Senate
Michigan Senate
Minnesota Senate and House
Mississippi Senate and House
Missouri House
Montana House
Nevada Senate and Assembly
New Mexico House
Oregon House
South Carolina House
South Dakota Senate and House
Texas Senate
Utah Senate and House
Virginia House
West Virginia Senate and House

Presiding Officer or Other Leader

Arizona Senate and House	Missouri Senate
Connecticut House	Nebraska Senate
Delaware House	New Jersey Senate and Assembly
Georgia House	New York Senate and Assembly
Hawaii House	Oklahoma Senate and House
Indiana Senate and House	Pennsylvania House
Iowa Senate	Puerto Rico Senate
Kentucky House	Washington Senate
Michigan House	Wyoming Senate and House

Rules or Calendaring Committee

Alaska Senate and House	North Carolina House
Colorado House	Ohio Senate and House
Florida Senate and House	South Carolina Senate
Illinois Senate and House	Tennessee Senate and House
Iowa House	Texas House
Kansas Senate and House	Washington House
Montana Senate	Wisconsin Senate and House[18]

In addition to the regular calendar of business, many legislatures have additional calendars to expedite legislation, such as consent calendars for noncontroversial bills and special order or rules calendars to expedite consideration of major legislation.[19] It is important to know how each house in your legislature works.

If a piece of library legislation is sponsored by the individual responsible for the priority order of all legislation, chances are high that it will be heard expeditiously. If the person in charge of setting the daily calendar for hearing a bill on general file does not like the bill, sometimes it will stay on general file until the cutoff date for debating legislation. Therefore, just because a bill made it out of committee, even with a unanimous "aye" vote, a single individual can kill it by simply not scheduling it for debate. If the library legislation can get on a consent calendar, it passes through easier and possibly without changes. Knowledge of these procedures is essential in shepherding a bill through the process.

Amending Bills

A third consideration is how your state amends bills. Many states, such as Oregon and North Dakota, do not allow amendments after the bill leaves the committee.[20] This means that the most important lobbying efforts take place before the debate in the house or senate.

Sponsoring libraries must know the rules of the assembly, house, and senate regarding amendments so that they are at the right place at the right time and do not wait too long before attempting to make changes or fight changes that were made unexpectedly. Sponsoring a bill in states that only allow floor amendments can be very frustrating. At least when a bill is amended in a committee, there is a possibility that librarians can testify for or against it. But when a library bill is amended on the floor of the house, assembly, or senate, librarians can only hope that the sponsors are well-prepared for the battle. It is often frustrating to sit in the gallery watching debate, knowing the answers to the questions presented or knowing how to fight a particular amendment, and not be able to communicate with the legislator who is on the spot.

States differ on how floor amendments are handled if they are allowed. In some states, major floor amendments may be offered without advance notice, and sometimes without sufficient time for other legislators to even "plug in" the amendment.[21] Other states attempt to control amendments by restricting them to a certain order of business, by requiring prefiling of amendments and written analyses of what an amendment does, and by utilizing a video screen to display the amendments. Three-quarters of the legislatures restrict the offering of floor amendments to a particular order of business, usually second reading.[22] Twelve states require written analyses for all floor amendments, while twenty-seven additional states require them for amendments to specific types of bills.[23]

The librarian-lobbyist must know and understand the amending process so that the library legislation he or she supports does not get amended without support of the library community and so that the librarian does not lose the opportunity to offer an amendment because the amending time period passed or the amendment was not prefiled, or because an analysis had not been prepared.

Many, many additional legislative procedures exist about which the library lobbyist needs to be informed. A paid lobbyist is usually aware of the potential problem areas and will alert local librarians about the timeliness of letters and calls supporting or decrying amendments or other problems. It is nevertheless a good idea for the politically active librarian to be on top of the process in the state legislature, as small procedural "glitches" can sometimes kill a bill inadvertently.

Developing a Statewide Plan of Action

In General

Passing legislation at the state level takes a great deal of planning and lead time. An individual librarian cannot do it alone. Instead, a legislative committee of the state library association usually plans possible legislative efforts. The committee will most likely take its plan to an annual meeting of the membership or poll the membership by mail if the timing is not appropriate. If the association generally adopts the committee's platforms or recommendations, then the committee—in cooperation with the library leadership, the state library, and the library lobbyist—must organize a campaign.

A statewide coordinated campaign takes a great deal of effort and thought, but if the initiative is important enough, it should receive a lot of support from local librarians. If the resources are available, a very effective technique is to distribute a legislative information packet to all librarians in the state. The packet would contain a copy of the bill, an analysis of what the bill does, a timetable for the local librarians to follow, specific brochures or information to distribute to legislators representing their district, and a list of recommendations on how to lobby locally (or a copy of this book!).

Whoever is in charge at the state level must be extremely well-organized to make sure that all legislators are contacted by their local librarians if possible. In most states, the legislative session begins sometime in January. (See Table 4.)[24]

The optimum time to contact legislators in the states whose sessions begin in January is in mid-November or early December. It is important to avoid the holidays in planning, but do not wait to contact legislators until the week before the session begins when so many groups remember that the time is suddenly at hand.

Pre-Legislative Session Meeting

A very effective way to lobby legislators for a bill at this time is to arrange a meeting with the local librarians and the state legislators to go over the proposed legislation the librarians want. A lunch or dinner meeting is appropriate although not always possible.

Table 4 Legislative Sessions

State	Regular Session Beginning Date and Length	Can Regular Session Be Extended? By Whom?	Special Sessions? Called By Whom?
Alabama	Jan, Feb or Apr – varies during 4-year term; 105 calendar days	No	Yes – Governor
Alaska	Jan – 120 calendar days	Yes – Legislature	Yes – Governor or Legislature
Arizona	Jan – 100 days	Yes – Legislature	Yes – Governor or Legislature
Arkansas	Jan – odd, 60 calendar days (biennial session)	Yes – Legislature	Yes – Governor
California	Jan – odd through Nov – even	No	Yes – Governor
Colorado	Jan – odd, no limit; even, 140 days	Odd, Yes; Even, No	Yes – Governor or Legislature
Connecticut	Jan–Jun – odd; Feb–May – even	No	Yes – Governor or Legislature/ Sec. of State veto session
Delaware	Jan – 50 legislative days	Yes – Leg. Leadership	Yes – Leadership
Florida	Apr – 60 calendar days	Yes – Legislature	Yes – Governor, Leaders, poll of Membership
Georgia	Jan – 40 legislative days	No	Seldom – Governor or Legislature
Hawaii	Jan – 60 legislative days	Yes – Governor or Leg.	Yes – Governor or Legislature
Idaho	Jan – approx. 3 months	Yes	Yes – Governor
Illinois	Jan – approx. 6 months	Yes	Yes – Governor or Leadership
Indiana	Jan – odd, 61 days; even, 31 days	No	Yes – Governor
Iowa	Jan – to adjournment	No	Yes – Governor or Legislature
Kansas	Jan – odd, no limit; even, 90 calendar days	Odd, No; Even, Yes	Seldom – Governor
Kentucky	Jan – even, 60 legislative days (biennial session)	No	Yes – Governor
Louisiana	Mar – 85 calendar days	No	Yes – Governor or Legislature
Maine	Dec–Jun – odd; Jan–Apr – even	Yes – Legislature	Yes – Governor or Legislature
Maryland	Jan – 90 calendar days	Yes – Legislature	Yes – Governor
Massachusetts	Jan–Jan	N/A	Yes – Governor or Legislature
Michigan	Jan–Dec	N/A	Seldom – Governor
Minnesota	Jan–May each year; 120-legislative day limit during biennium	No	Yes – Governor
Mississippi	Jan – 125 days 1st year of term; 90 days other 3 yrs.	Yes – Legislature	Yes – Governor
Missouri	Jan–Jun – odd; Jan–May – even	No	Yes – Governor
Montana	Jan – odd, 90 legislative days (biennial session)	No	Yes – Governor or Legislature
Nebraska	Jan – odd, 90 legislative days; even, 60 leg. days	Yes – Legislature	Yes – Governor or Legislature
Nevada	Jan – odd, 5–6 months (biennial session)	N/A	Seldom – Governor
New Hampshire	Jan – 45 legislative days	Yes – Leadership/Gov.	Yes – Governor or Leadership
New Jersey	Jan – continuous	N/A	Yes – Governor or Leadership
New Mexico	Jan – odd, 60 calendar days; even 30 cal. days	No	Yes – Governor or Legislature
New York	Jan–Jun	Yes	Yes – Governor or Leadership
North Carolina	Jan – to adjournment	N/A	Yes – Governor or Legislature
North Dakota	Jan – odd, 80 legislative days (biennial session)	No	Seldom – Governor
Ohio	Jan – odd, 6 months; even, 3 months	N/A	Yes – Governor or Leadership
Oklahoma	Jan – 90 legislative days	No	Yes – Governor or Legislature
Oregon	Jan – odd, 6 months (biennial session)	N/A	Seldom – Governor
Pennsylvania	Jan–Nov	No	Yes – Governor or Leadership
Rhode Island	Jan – 60 legislative days	Yes – Leadership/Gov.	Yes – Governor
South Carolina	Jan–Jun	Yes – Legislature	Yes – Governor
South Dakota	Jan – odd, 40 legislative days; even, 35 leg. days	No	Yes – Governor
Tennessee	Jan – 90 legislative days over biennium	No	Yes – Governor or Legislature
Texas	Jan – odd, 140 calendar days (biennial session)	No	Yes – Governor
Utah	Jan – 45 calendar days	No	Yes – Governor
Vermont	Jan – approx. 4 months	N/A	Yes – Governor
Virginia	Jan – odd, 30 calendar days; even, 60 cal. days	Yes – Legislature	Yes – Governor or Legislature
Washington	Jan – odd, 105 calendar days; even, 60 cal. days	Yes – Governor or Leg.	Yes – Governor or Legislature
West Virginia	Jan – 60 calendar days	Yes – Governor or Leg.	Yes – Governor or Legislature
Wisconsin	Jan – begins odd year, runs 2 years	Yes – Jt.Comm.Leg.Org. /Jt.Res.	Yes – Governor
Wyoming	Jan – odd, 40 legislative days; even, 20 leg. days	No	Yes – Governor

October 28, 1992

The Honorable John Vinich
P. O. Box 248
Elksburg, WY 82070

PUBLIC LIBRARY

Dear John:

This letter is to confirm the date of the library's annual legislative dinner scheduled for November 14, at 6:00 p.m. at the
High Street Restaurant. We always appreciate our legislators'
willingness to attend these meetings so that we can exchange
information on any issues which might affect libraries in the upcoming session.

My secretary called all legislators with alternative dates last
week and everyone can make it on the 14th. Please let me know
if you have a change of plans between now and then.

I look forward to our meeting. Please come with questions
and any information you might have concerning potential library
legislation.

Thanks!

Sincerely,

Ruth Poe, Director
Elksburg Public Library

A meeting before the legislative session begins reminds
legislators about proposed library bills.

It is important to arrange a time at which the legislators can be
relaxed enough to listen carefully. It is also important to allow time
for an informal chat prior to the meeting. Often the best lobbying
can be done at an informal session on a one-on-one basis where
the legislator can ask dumb questions without everyone's knowing
about it.

A legislative packet similar to the one the legislative committee
gives to local libraries is extremely useful. If the librarian can send
this information to legislators prior to the meeting, the legislator
will have time to read and prepare. Remember to take additional
copies to the meeting because not all legislators will remember to

bring the packet sent to them. At the meeting, if possible, distribute an information sheet specifically targeting the effect of the bill on the legislator's home community and constituency. It will keep the legislators interested in the meeting and in the bill. Either a local librarian who is well-informed about the legislation or a member of the legislative committee should make a short presentation about the proposed legislation and how it would specifically affect the legislator's community. Time should be allowed for questions and answers after the presentation.

If the librarians hold an early meeting (not one right before a session begins), it is important to follow up with a card, note, or information sheet again right before the legislator leaves for the session, such as after Christmas but before the new year. Legislators are inundated at this time with requests for appearances and meetings, so they are pleased to receive only a reminder card from those groups and individuals who have already done their initial contacting and educating.

If you ask a legislator to attend a meeting, make sure that the legislator's role in the meeting is very clear in the invitation. For example, if the meeting is held during the political campaign season and all candidates are invited to speak about the library legislation, the candidates should know that it is a political format. If an incumbent is asked to speak during the political season, make it clear ahead of time that his or her purpose is to impart the kind of valuable information an elected official has, not to campaign for re-election. If the purpose of the meeting is to educate legislators about the bill, let them know they will not be put on the spot but rather that they will receive input from their librarians as constituents. If the meeting is right before the session, but the librarians want to discuss the legislators' stands on a variety of issues, let the legislator's know that as well. Although most legislators are great "on their feet," they appreciate the courtesy of knowing what to expect ahead of time.

Timetable

Of primary importance is a timetable for local librarians to follow as the bill is written, sent to potential sponsors for approval, rewritten by the state legislative service office, and eventually introduced. The legislative committee or librarian-lobbyist in charge of the lobbying effort should write this document. The timetable is distributed to all librarians, politically active or not, and periodically updated. It should contain to the extent possible the days that the local librarians need to act. For instance, many state library associations hold "Legislative Days" at the capitol building where librarians from all over the state go to the capitol and discuss pending library issues and other library concerns with their legislators. This is an easy day to predict. Not so easy to predict is the best time to flood the capitol with letters of support for a certain bill or amendment. The process moves so fast and is sometimes so erratic that sending letters of support needs to be something that every librarian is "on call" to do.

Letters to a Standing Committee

Once a bill is introduced, it is good practice to encourage all librarians in the state to write the members of the committee to which the bill was assigned urging its passage. It is especially important that the librarians from the districts represented by the committee members write them. A letter from home often holds a lot more weight with legislators than several from other individuals who are concerned but who are not primary constituents.

February 28, 1992

The Honorable Robert Reese
Senate Education Committee
State Capitol Building
Cheyenne, WY 82002

PUBLIC LIBRARY

Dear Senator Reese:

You will soon be hearing Senate File 102, Library Districts, sponsored by Senator John Vinich, in your Education Committee. I would certainly appreciate your favorable consideration of this bill in your committee. The library district bill allows citizens to vote to tax themselves for library services. If a library district is created, it would provide the poorer libraries in the state sufficient funding to continue to provide library services. Without it, you may see several libraries severely curtail their services.

It is an important bill for the entire senate to debate since some of the districts which need this bill most are not represented on your committee. Voting this bill out of committee is extremely

important, and I thank you sincerely for your efforts in seeing
that it receives sufficient votes to get it out of committee.
Please feel free to contact me if you need additional information. Thanks again for your help.

Sincerely,

Ruth Poe, Director
Elksburg Public Library

Letters from primary constituents to members
of a standing committee are especially effective.

A bill is not usually heard immediately upon reaching the committee (although sometimes it can happen within a day or so!), so
the organizing librarian could give local librarians a week or more
to send letters to this committee depending on the calendar of the
particular legislature. The committee is the first and sometimes the
hardest hurdle to overcome in passing a bill. If the committee members receive a lot of public input about a bill, they will pay more
attention to the bill than if they had received none. The bill is more
likely to get out of committee if the committee believes the bill is
popular and has statewide support.

Attending Meetings
of the Standing Committee

Whoever is organizing the statewide effort must also decide, along
with the sponsors of the bill, who should testify to the committee,
how many individuals should be there, and how long a general presentation should take. A legislator has a harder time voting against
a bill if several primary constituents who support the legislation
are sitting in the same room. Legislatures usually meet during the
day, and more often than not the ordinary citizen or constituents do
not have the time to attend hearings or meetings. Personal appearance is therefore a tremendously powerful tool. When librarians,
trustees, and friends from the districts of the committee members
attend committee meetings at which the discussion and vote on a
bill take place, their legislators will take note. However, the legislator must know beforehand that the constituents are there, even
if they do not testify. If the librarian has lobbied well up to this

point, the legislator will know the librarian's face. Even so, the librarian should still let the legislator know he or she is there before the meeting begins. It just keeps a legislator "clean" to have constituents watching the process. An age-old legislative joke is that people should never watch sausage or laws being made. In many ways it is true: a lot of bills pass or fail for no good reason, and if the public at large became more involved with the process, legislators might be forced to approach their jobs differently. Obviously, different legislatures have different procedures, but, in general, the public unfortunately is not deeply involved in lobbying most bills.

Statewide Lobbying Action

Once the bill has successfully passed out of committee with a "do-pass" recommendation, it is time for all librarians in the state to become active once again. At this time, all librarians should send letters to their legislators as soon as possible. The legislators who voted favorably on the legislation to get it out of committee do not need to receive a second letter of support unless the librarian includes new information. The committee members should receive thank-you notes from their home constituents immediately after a successful committee vote.

In addition to the sponsors of the bill, there will be the proponents of the legislation on the floor. They will often be committee members who state that in committee they heard from twenty librarians (or whatever) who told the committee such and so. It helps to let all legislators, but especially the committee members, know early and often that you appreciated their support. Those committee members who voted against the bill should receive letters from constituents in their county urging their support.

A lobbyist, by the way, can be helpful in all of the foregoing steps. Someone needs to be at the capitol, monitoring or watchdogging the legislation. When it is assigned to a certain committee, the lobbyist or person in charge needs to contact the appropriate librarians and request action. The librarians must be informed about when and where any proposed hearings will be held. Once the bill is out of committee and on general file, the lobbyist must find out when it will be debated so that the appropriate librarians can be alerted. If a lobbyist is not available, the librarian in charge of legislative matters (usually the chair or a member of the state library association legislative committee) must call the capitol building every day and ask the status of the bill in question, what hearings are

March 4, 1992

Senator Liz Byrd
Education Committee
Senate Chambers
State Capitol Building
Cheyenne, WY 82002

PUBLIC LIBRARY

Dear Senator Byrd:

This is just a quick note to let you know how much I appreciated your favorable vote in committee on Senator Vinich's senate file 102, "Library Districts." Your comments regarding the need for library services were astute and accurate. The librarians across the state are aware of your efforts and appreciate your support greatly.

Thanks again for your vote and efforts on behalf of this bill. Any help you could give the bill on the floor of the senate would also be appreciated.

Sincerely,

Ruth Poe, Director
Elksburg Public Library

Reward decision makers every step of the way.

scheduled for that day, and what bills the committee responsible for the library bill is hearing.

The best way to ensure passage before the debate begins is to have the sponsor or sponsors of the bill take a "nose count" of legislators in support of the legislation. By this time, the lobbyist in charge should have received from the local librarians a list of strong "yes" votes, strong "no" votes, and swing votes. The legislative sponsor needs this information to verify the count. An important kind of lobbying at this point comes from the sponsor or sponsors of the bill. Although most states prohibit legislators from trading votes, sponsors will discuss important bills with other lawmakers, especially with the swing votes, to try to convince them that the bill is worthy of support.

Legislators lobbying each other is an extremely powerful persuasive technique. Legislators have only so much "legislative capital" (the ability to obtain commitments from fellow legislators), and the sponsors may not be willing to spend it on a library bill. If they encourage their colleagues to vote favorably on every bill they sponsor, the other legislators will stop listening and stop responding. If they ask for a commitment on one or two bills a session, they might get it. Good or bad, legislators will often vote one way or another because of the sponsor of the bill and not because of the merits of the bill. Local librarians should encourage their legislators to do some private lobbying.

In any case, the sponsor should at least be willing to do a head count of fellow legislators so that the librarian-lobbyist has an idea of how much work has to be done. If the librarians in the state have done the appropriate work and received enough commitments from their legislators to pass the bill, everyone will know the results of the vote before the debate even begins. When this happens, the debate is usually for the purpose of generating press for hometown newspapers or placing legislators' support of the issue on record for future reference. If the librarian-lobbyist is unable to determine the vote before the floor debate begins, then the debate must be monitored closely.

Legislative Debate

It is extremely important to have someone listen to the floor debate, to document votes on each reading and on each amendment, and to get a record of official votes. In fact, librarians may want to tape-record the floor debate, even if the debate is officially recorded, unless copies or transcripts of that debate are available immediately. The recording is valuable for many reasons. First, it is difficult for even the best of listeners to remember exactly what each legislator says about a bill. If time is available between votes, the tape can be transcribed or at least listened to again so that nonsupportive legislators' quotes and information can be given to the appropriate local librarian for lobbying purposes. If a legislator receives a series of questions that were hard for the lobbyist to catch, a recording will be valuable. Finally, after the session, the statewide library publication can use the recording to print quotes from individual legislators about the library legislation efforts.

The lobbyist should be very familiar with the rules regarding voice votes, recorded votes, time to vote if electronic voting is available, and ways that legislators can kill a bill. For example, it is difficult to determine how each legislator voted if only a voice vote is required on any of the readings. The lobbyist will want to discuss with the sponsor the possibility of asking for a *division* on a voice vote or a roll-call vote so that those individuals who do not support the bill or an amendment to it will be easier to ascertain. The lobbyist must be quick enough if it is a standing vote only to write down the nonsupportive legislators and get this information back to the library constituents. As mentioned previously, each legislature and most often each house in each legislature has its own rules that the lobbyist and sponsor can use to their advantage in assessing the support of the bill.

Questions are often asked during debate that the sponsors did not predict or cannot answer. If an informed individual is watchdogging the process, that person can either pass a note to the legislator with the answers or prepare an official written set of answers to distribute before the next reading of the bill. Someone must follow the debate carefully. If a misconception goes unanswered, it can sometimes kill an otherwise popular bill. The lobbyist must also know the rules of each house concerning amendments to a bill. There is much variation among legislatures on procedures for floor amendments. If an amendment must be prefiled or distributed twenty-four hours before introduction, the lobbyist has a little time to put an emergency calling tree into action. If the amendments can be made on the spot during debate and without distribution to anyone other than the legislators on the floor of the assembly, house, or senate, then the responsibility for killing or supporting the amendment often falls on the shoulders of the legislative sponsors.

The lobbyist and librarians throughout the state who are supporting a piece of legislation must always trust the sponsors in an emergency situation, even if they do not understand why the legislator is acting or voting in a particular manner. A legislator must use his or her own judgment about on-the-spot compromises to save the bill, even though to the library community the result looks possibly disastrous. A lot goes on behind the scenes in the legislature. For example, at one point I offered an amendment to a bill that provided funding for a new state library building. The person watchdogging the process did not contact me regarding my motives for offering the amendment, but instead called all members of the State Library Board, several of whom showed up quite alarmed in the lobby within two or three hours. They set the statewide telephone tree into action so that before long librarians throughout the state were calling me and other legislators and telling us to vote against my amendment. This reaction is an excellent example of poor lobbying.

If legislators are friendly to the library world, librarians should always query them about the motive or rationale behind a bill or amendment before "siccing" grass roots supporters on them. If a legislator is well-known for trying to sandbag library legislation, then there may well be reason to worry and querying is not required. Most often talking with that legislator will at least give the lobbyist additional information on how to fight the amendment, even if the discussion does not dissuade the legislator from introducing it. Or sometimes, as in my case, if a friendly legislator offers an amendment, give that person the benefit of the doubt. When I explained to the library board members what I was doing, they were satisfied that it was not a bad idea and that perhaps they had been misled by the lobbyist. Librarians cannot afford to make this kind of mistake too often, or with legislators who are not also librarians! It could give us a bad name!

Finally, the moment comes when the legislators make their last and most important vote on a bill (that is, if it survives the first two readings). If sufficient numbers of legislators vote for it, the library legislation will go on to the next house. If not, the bill is dead (although there are ways to raise a bill from the dead here, too!). Librarians should know the rules on how many votes are necessary to pass the bill. Most often it will take a simple majority, but there may be cases where it takes more.

A lobbyist should understand that a "no" vote does not necessarily mean that the legislator is opposed to the bill. For example, in most legislatures, if one house passes a bill and the other house makes changes that the first house does not like, a conference committee of members from each house will be selected to make compromises to take back to each house for approval. In the Wyoming legislature, conference committees are usually made up of two "yes" votes and one "no" vote from each house. Consequently, if a supporter of a library bill wants to get on a conference committee to effect its final outcome, sometimes that person will vote "no" on the bill, hoping to get a spot on the conference committee. In other cases, a supporter of a state aid to libraries bill may vote "no" if that person thinks that the funding level is too low. Under those circumstances, the legislator would vote "no" only if the bill had a sufficient number of votes to pass. Therefore, if a supporter seems to have jumped ship on a bill, before blasting that person in a library journal or newsletter, contact the legislator and ask for an explanation of the vote. Often, you may end up thanking instead of condemning that individual.

A related issue is that the rationale behind an amendment or bill is sometimes unclear without an explanation of intent from the sponsor. Instead of publicly attacking the bill, the amendment, or the sponsor, a good lobbyist will first attempt to talk to the sponsor or an aide. For example, I introduced a bill to raise legislators' pay, a good knee-jerk reaction bill for critics. An editor from a statewide newspaper called before he wrote an editorial to find out my reasoning. After a twenty-minute discussion, the editor wrote that a pay increase was necessary to keep a citizen's legislature viable in the future, and that I had a lot of gumption to offer a bill in the face of sure and intense criticism.[25] I appreciated his effort, as opposed to that of an editor from another statewide newspaper who did not contact me and who called the bill the "worst of the session"!

After a bill passes the first house, it must go through the same procedure on the other side. Everything from letter writing by local librarians to testifying and watchdogging floor debate must take place again. There are so many places and ways a bill could die that the effort to pass one gets extremely frustrating. The person in charge of the statewide effort to pass a bill and the library community must build up a lot of stamina in their lobbying efforts and realize that passing a bill is time-consuming and tricky.

Bill Reaches Governor

Once the bill passes both houses, it then must be scrutinized for legality and constitutionality by the state attorney general and signed by the governor. Sometimes the most frustrating way to lose a bill is to have the attorney general in his or her review and recommendation to the governor determine that the bill was not worded correctly, that it is ambiguous, that it was inserted in the wrong part of the statutes, or that it is unconstitutional. After the bill passes the final legal scrutiny of the attorney general, under certain circumstances, it may be time for the library world to contact the governor if there is any possibility of a veto.

The primary sponsor or sponsors of the bill know best how to approach the governor. In some cases, it is better to do nothing and trust that, since the bill was popular among legislators and it does what it is supposed to do, the governor will not veto it. On the other hand, if there has been some controversy around the bill or if the vote was close, librarians may want to determine how the governor feels about the bill. Sometimes a legislative liaison can provide this information to the sponsors. The sponsor may want to speak with the governor, although some states prohibit a governor from revealing a veto decision before it is made. If it appears that the bill may be vetoed, the statewide library community should once again go into action. A mass mailing to the governor in support of a piece of legislation is effective, or if time is short, librarians can send faxes or telegrams of support to the governor's office. The lobbyist and the legislative sponsors need to strategize and plan the most appropriate course of action.

The final critical leg of a successful bill's passage is developing the implementing rules and regulations as discussed earlier. Not until they are solidly in place should the librarians in the state sit back and pat themselves on the back.

Killing a Bill

Although the focus of the above discussion has been on passing legislation, the library community may want to kill legislation at times. Librarians can use many of the same techniques to kill legislation that they would to pass it. In fact, it is often easier for a legislator to vote "no" on a bill than to vote "yes," because a "no" vote will often protect the status quo, with which everyone is familiar. Even though maintaining the status quo may result in problems, they are familiar problems. Generally, legislators and legislatures have a harder time with unknown, unproved, and untested ideas than with the older imperfect yet familiar ideas. An adage legislators often state is that if it is a good enough idea, it will be back again.

Key words for passing a bill are *emergency, timely, forefront, well-thought out,* and *necessary.* Key phrases to kill a bill are *if it ain't broke, don't fix it; it's been this way for the last fifty years, why change now; results are uncertain;* and *costs too much.*

The Follow-Up

Instead of immediately celebrating their hard work and good fortune in passing or killing a bill affecting libraries, the library community should first get out their pens and start sending as many thank-you notes as they did original letters. When legislators are responsive to their electorate, it is important to reward them for that behavior. On many issues, a legislator will not receive even a postcard from anyone in support of or against a piece of legislation. When the legislator receives many letters and lots of input on a piece of legislation, it is gratifying and unusual if the legislator also receives the same number of cards thanking him or her for the positive vote.

The person in charge of the statewide lobbying network should prepare press releases for local librarians to fill in the blanks and take to their local newspapers. This is probably the most valuable feedback a legislator can receive. Many legislators are career legislators and plan to run again. A story about their legislative actions written by an organization not associated with them is valuable to the legislators and credible to the public. Being a legislator is tough work with very little reward. It is always gratifying to have a group thank legislators publicly for the hard work they did on a bill.

The lobbyist should also contact the editor of the state library newsletter or publication to give him or her a story or an interview. The library publication can handle legislative news in a variety of ways. It can print votes on key bills; it can print outcomes of key bills and their sponsors; it can print excerpts from floor debate; it can give legislators a "rating"; or it can simply summarize the legislation. If the publication is sent to all legislators, the stories on the outcome of the session should be handled carefully because legislators are more likely to read the publication immediately after the session than at any other time during the year. Remember, legislators like to see their names in print in a positive manner or connected with a bill on which they worked. If their names are left out, it may sour them on future efforts.

The editor must also avoid other potential pitfalls. For example, if the statewide publication prints a list of how legislators voted on a number of key bills, it should also print the bill title or topic: "State Aid to Public Libraries" instead of H.B. 141. Where only the votes and the bill number are listed, readers will not know what the legislators were voting on, and the deletion may anger legislators. Without the appropriate information, constituents around the state cannot independently decide if the legislator voted correctly.

Further, as discussed previously, a "no" vote is not always indicative of nonsupport. Whoever compiles the list of votes to include in an article should try to note any peculiar or atypical votes on the part of a legislator and, if possible, print an explanation. The drawback is that every legislator listed will request space to explain his or her vote if one legislator is allowed to do it. At the very least, a legislator who is contacted about a peculiar vote will be pleased to explain his or her vote and to be informed about the impending publication. That legislator can write a letter to the editor if he or she believes it is important to explain the vote. In addition, a "yes" vote is not always indicative of support. The same legislators who vote in favor of a bill may have voted against every favorable amendment to it or may have added a detrimental amendment.

When the editor includes a list of legislators to thank specially, it is important that all supportive legislators are included. A conscientious lobbyist will have this information, although sometimes the stars of the backroom lobbying among legislators themselves are hard to discern. Whoever writes the article should contact local librarians regarding their legislator's support if it is unclear.

Sometimes professional organizational journals or publications from businesses or other groups print excerpts from floor debate. This is usually not a problem in terms of accuracy if the debate is recorded and is public record. If the quotes come from someone listening in the gallery or elsewhere, it is essential to get an accurate and official rendition. In fact, if the lobbyist has recorded the floor debate as suggested earlier, then it will be easy to satisfy any challenge. Not all legislators are orators and sometimes they do not mean what they say or say what they mean.

Selective quotes can cause problems. A quote taken out of context of an entire debate can mean something different from what the legislator intended and different from what the other legislators understood. Whoever writes the article should be sensitive to the meaning, especially if the article is written to show a legislator's nonsupport of library legislation.

Occasionally a publication will "rate" or "grade" legislators on their votes. This practice is very dangerous. No one likes to get a poor grade! Giving a legislator a poor grade will not persuade that person to vote in favor of library legislation next time. In fact, it may sour the legislator on libraries. It may dissuade some groups from voting for the legislator during the next election,[26] but the electorate has a short memory, and even a poor rating may help the legislator's name recognition.

It is good to recognize your supportive legislators because organizations often forget to do this. If the statewide association gives an annual award to the most supportive legislator, make sure that the selection process is clear and that the others who are nominated are also mentioned. Legislators know which legislators have done what in certain areas. When they see a legislator receive an award from a group in an area in which they have done more work than the award recipient, they are not pleased with the group giving the award. Librarians giving awards should make sure the process of nomination and selection is clear and understandable to avoid these kinds of problems.

Notes

1. American Library Association, *The ALA Yearbook of Library and Information Services: A Review of Library Events 1989,* vol. 15 (Chicago: American Library Association, 1990), 264.

2. Ibid., 271.

3. Ibid., 275.

4. Ibid., 281.

5. Ibid., 290.

6. Marilyn Gell Mason, "Politics and the Public Library: A Management Guide," *Library Journal* 114 (15 March 1989): 27.

7. Alice Ihrig, "Lobbying," in *Funding Alternatives for Libraries,* eds. Patricia Senn Breivik and E. Burr Gibson (Chicago: American Library Association, 1979), 97.

8. Ibid.

9. Ihrig also recommends this type of professional identification. Ibid., 99.

10. Ibid., 94.

11. Ibid., 95.

12. National Conference of State Legislatures, *Inside the Legislative Process; A Comprehensive Survey of the American Society of Legislative Clerks and Secretaries in Cooperation With the National Conference of State Legislatures* (Denver: National Conference of State Legislatures, 1988), 5.

13. Ibid.

14. Ibid., 57.

15. Ibid.

16. Ibid.

17. Ibid., 5–6.

18. Ibid., 6–7.

19. Ibid., 7.

20. Ibid.

21. The Wyoming senate has no rules governing how long an amendment must be on a legislator's desk before the senate votes on it.

22. Ibid., 9.

23. Ibid., 12.

24. "1991 Legislative Session Calendar," *State Legislatures* 17 (January 1991): 2.

25. Kerry Drake, "Wyoming Must Re-Examine Legislative Pay," *The Wyoming Eagle*, 3 January 1991.

26. The most effective lobbying group in Wyoming that gives out grades before an election for single-issue voters to use in deciding their votes is the National Rifle Association, as might be expected. Members receive the candidate's grades right before election, and many use them to fill out their ballot. Voters concerned about other emotional issues, such as right-to-life versus choice, often use a preelection grading system when it is available.

6

Do's and Don'ts
of Lobbying

Universal Experiences in Lobbying

This book examines lobbying techniques at the local, state, and national level. Each type of lobbying effort is slightly different and requires slightly different planning. Even so, some kinds of interactions occur at every level of lobbying, and the accompanying rules of etiquette need to be followed by everyone interested in effectively communicating with their decision makers. Many writers frame the etiquette of these universal experiences in lists of do's and don'ts.[1] It is wise to follow these suggestions, and it is fun to hear examples of blunders. This chapter deals with etiquette tips to follow and goofs to avoid when dealing with decision makers—local, state, or federal. Some tips will be more appropriate for one level of lobbying than another, but in general they are good advice for the novice as well as the more seasoned librarian-lobbyist.

Do's of Lobbying Etiquette

Universal Basics

Common themes run through literature on lobbying etiquette. These themes reinforce my own list of do's developed over the years through experience on the receiving end as the "lobbee." My list requires lobbyists to be truthful, accurate, courteous, concise, and brief. Although it sounds simplistic to encourage a librarian-lobbyist to abide by these words, it is astounding how often lobbyists, professional and lay, make mistakes in these areas.

TRUTHFULNESS AND ACCURATE INFORMATION

It is easy to "forget" to tell the decision maker about one little drawback to a bill. Even if it is insignificant when first forgotten, it gains importance by its absence. Using last year's figures or guessing at numbers you do not know is always tempting and often done! When a legislator uses the inaccurate information you gave him or her, not only does the legislator lose credibility with other legislators, the library loses credibility with the legislators. If decision makers cannot depend on information from a librarian, what and whom *can* they trust? Information is our business.

COURTEOUSNESS

Even though elected officials are public servants, the lobbying public does not have the right to treat them rudely; being courteous to decision makers is essential, even if it is difficult.

CONCISENESS AND BREVITY

Finally, in a political world of limited time and multiple issues, decision makers not only like but also are more likely to remember a concise and brief letter, phone call, conversation, issue statement, or communication of any kind.

What the Experts Say

In 1988, Jacklyn H. Ducote polled legislators from all over the United States, asking for specific do's and don'ts of lobbying as well as tips about how to lobby effectively.[2] The survey included responses from 124 legislators and lobbyists from forty states. She determined that the main themes from the responses were knowledge and honesty. The top three do's from this survey mirror my own observations and are listed below:

1. Know your issue and provide accurate and timely information; answer all questions and prepare your arguments well. These do's were recommended by thirty-seven legislators and forty-nine lobbyists.
2. Be honest and straightforward; tell the truth and be credible. These do's were recommended by twenty-three legislators and thirty-three lobbyists.
3. Make your comments brief, concise, and to the point. This do was recommended by fifteen legislators and seven lobbyists.

These are all good recommendations. A more thorough discussion of several of these points is necessary to illustrate how well-intentioned lobbyists sometimes inadvertently get into trouble.

First, knowing your issue is extremely important. If you do not know what you are trying to communicate or what you want, you will not likely be very successful in your efforts to obtain it. In order for the decision maker to support you or your issue, the decision maker has to know your goal, the issues, the background, and the arguments. A sponsor of your bill especially does not want to look dumb and spoil his or her credibility among the other decision makers. Make decision makers look good by providing them with good, accurate information they can depend on and use to impress and to persuade the other decision makers that the library issue is worthwhile. Before you can educate others about an issue, you must educate yourself.

To be an effective lobbyist, you have to be absolutely honest about an issue and its pros and cons. You do not want to put a legislator in the position of being embarrassed in debate or in committee because someone else brought up a weakness about your bill that you kept from the legislator. Being less than truthful will destroy your credibility with the decision maker so that when you want his or her support on another issue, you will get a resounding "no thanks."

Although you need to be thorough enough to provide full, relevant information, remember also to be as concise as possible in each interaction.

A good way to be both thorough and concise is to accompany the more extensive documents containing background information with a one-page summary. Often, the only thing a decision maker has time to read (or skim) is the summary. A summary is especially important if you have not provided all members of the decision-making body with all the information. One of the decision makers who received your packet may want to share the information with other decision makers. The one-page summary is easy to copy and will often be distributed. The decision maker will probably not have time to plow through pages of materials in order to glean from them the most important information to distribute to others.

Specific Tips

In addition to the top three do's of lobbying discussed above, legislators and lobbyists recommended a myriad of additional tips for the lobbyist.[3] Library trustee manuals, general lobbying books and articles, and other library-related lobbying articles also provide additional suggestions.[4] Keep these handy and read them before engaging in a major legislative effort. Meanwhile, take to heart the tips in the following etiquette guide for the lay lobbyist, compiled from personal experience and several excellent sources.[5]

BE APPRECIATIVE

Acknowledge past support and convey appreciation for any current action. Appreciation comes in many different forms. The librarian lobbyist should send thank-you notes after every interaction and after every positive statement the decision maker makes publicly. Write the note so that it both reinforces the library issue and thanks the decision maker for attending a meeting, supporting a bill, speaking during debate, making a public quote in favor of libraries, or anything else the decision maker might have done to support libraries.

If a decision maker sponsors a bill and spends a great deal of time fighting for it, it is appropriate to send flowers or other types of thanks to the chambers or to the decision maker's office in appreciation. Thank-you's can include letters to the editor, baked goods or other edibles sent to the chambers, a balloon bouquet with the library's name as prominent as the bouquet itself, a singing telegram, and whatever else a creative librarian can dream up. Although I have received or watched other legislators receive all of the above at one time or another, my observation is that decision makers perhaps like flowers or food best. Food distributed to legislators is often in their mouths before the acknowledgment envelope

March 7, 1992

The Honorable John Vinich
Senate Chambers
State Capitol Building
Cheyenne, WY 82002

Dear John:

    This is just a short note to thank you for your excellent presentation of the library district bill on the floor of the senate yesterday. Your answer in response to the comment that authorization of districts is just another tax increase was articulate and stated well. As you mentioned, authorization for a public referendum cannot be equated with raising people's taxes.
    I also thought your point regarding the inherent unfairness of geographic location driving the quality of library services in the state was especially effective. I know this hit home with other senators from those areas without a strong tax base.
    Thanks again for everything you have done to help this bill along. I hope it makes it through third reading tomorrow. I will be in the balcony if you need additional information or help from me.
    Best wishes.

Sincerely,

Ruth Poe, Director
Elksburg Public Library

A thank-you letter is always appropriate.

is opened. Therefore, when delivering food, make sure that the library's name is prominent on the tray so the decision makers have to eat around it!

BE POSITIVE

This is good advice, even if you lose, or perhaps *especially* if you lose. A common statement among decision makers is that if an idea is good enough, it will be back. If a bill has enough support, it will rise again. Decision makers remember the sore loser more than the failed bill or ordinance. A positive, smiling face garners more support and votes than a demanding, sulky countenance. When a legislator tells you that he or she does not support your bill, write a note thanking the legislator for being honest and straightforward. This is not to say that a lobbyist cannot feel frustrated, disappointed, angry, or disgruntled. It just means that the lobbyist cannot show these emotions to the decision maker! Go home and bake bread, punching out the decision makers in the dough, and then send the bread to the decision makers with a nice message that you appreciated their consideration of your bill this year and that you hope they will pass it next year.

When testifying before a committee on which I sit, one lobbyist sneered when asked questions, answered some questions sarcastically, refused to answer other questions, and generally came across as a very disagreeable person. When asked about her demeanor (after the committee), she indicated that she was so emotionally involved with the issue that she had not realized she was acting in such a manner. If a lobbyist is this emotionally involved, he or she should probably play a less active role in the actual presentations before decision makers. A negative posture, regardless of how good the reason for the negativism might be, does not help the effort.

ASK, DO NOT DEMAND

This is an interesting do because a lot of lobbyists, especially unexperienced lay lobbyists, do not understand the fine line between asking and demanding. Decision makers receive many letters starting with the phrase, "As a taxpayer, I demand that you . . . " or "As a taxpayer, I think you had better . . . " They end the letter with, "and if you do not vote this way, I will make sure that you are never elected in this district again." Decision makers know that everyone is a taxpayer, so this statement can be deleted. Threatening not to reelect them is also ineffective because decision makers react defensively. The purpose of lobbying is to be effective, not to "unload" on a decision maker.

The good library lobbyist will phrase a letter so that it gives the decision maker an opportunity to respond without feeling defensive or being put on the spot.

Demands draw lines and dare decision makers to step over them. Requests for support, in contrast, are extremely effective. The worst that can happen is that the legislator will say "no." If a lobbyist demands something and gets a "no," then the lobbyist is placed in the position of following through on whatever threat he or she had used in the original demand. Avoid boxing yourself into a corner. Asking never hurts; demanding usually defeats.

March 4, 1992

The Honorable Robert Reese
Senate Chambers
State Capitol Building
Cheyenne, WY 82002

Dear Senator Reese:

I want to let you know that I did not appreciate your "no" vote in committee on Senate File 102, Library Districts. If you had read the bill closely, you would have noticed that this is not an automatic tax increase! It is an optional increase in taxes on which the citizens of the districts must vote before it becomes effective. If people are willing to tax themselves for additional services, why not let them? I really thought your rationale stunk.

Luckily, you have plenty of time to change your mind before the bill is voted on by the whole senate. I hope that by the time it comes up that you will have reached your senses. Remember, librarians in your town vote, and they will remember your "no" vote next time they are in the voting booth.

Sincerely,

Ruth Poe, Director
Elksburg Public Library

Angry letters demand an apology. (See page 102.)

MAKE SURE YOU HAVE THE RIGHT LEGISLATOR
BEFORE THANKING OR CURSING HIM OR HER

Many legislators have similar names. It is essential for a librarian-lobbyist to tell the grass roots librarians the exact name of a legislator targeted for response. For example, a legislator in the Wyoming senate is named Kinnison. Senator Kinnison led the effort to cut an agency's budget. Within an hour of Kinnison's remarks on the floor, I had received two letters and several calls asking me what I was doing to the agency's budget. Soon a representative from the governor's office called me out of session, and we surmised that an observer had passed the wrong name to supporters. Be sure to enunciate carefully the name of the legislator you are targeting for anything!

March 6, 1992

The Honorable Robert Reese
Senate Chambers
State Capitol Building
Cheyenne, WY 82002

Dear Senator Reese:

   I want to again let you know how sorry I am that I wrote you a letter when I was angry. I was really out of line, and I apologize. I do want to try to explain my position again, however. Perhaps we could get together in the next couple of days so that I can personally answer any questions which you still have about the bill.

   As a result of our funding base, it will take our county twenty years to pay off a 1.3 million dollar library. Your county built a 3 million dollar library out of general funds. Our library serves the same number of people as yours, but our library has one-third fewer dollars to do it. The salaries of our library workers are on the average $4 less per hour than yours; we have no retirement benefits at all. One mill in your county equals $1.6 million. One mill in ours raises $95,000. We need your help on this bill to let the people in our county tax themselves for additional library service. Your county does not need this bill, and we wish we did not.

   Please help us. Your "aye" vote means a great deal to us and will not hurt your constituents at all. Thanks for your consideration. I will be calling you shortly to see if we can discuss any additional problems you might have with this bill.

Sincerely,

Ruth Poe, Director
Elksburg Public Library

An apology is an appropriate way to set relations straight.

REMEMBER, AN ENEMY ON ONE ISSUE
WILL BE A FRIEND ON ANOTHER

This is one of the most fascinating aspects of politics that lobbyists need to understand. A good decision maker cannot afford to carry a grudge or to berate another decision maker about a vote, because an enemy on one issue may be a friend on the next. For example, legislators make hundreds of votes on different issues during a session. Unless an issue divides along strictly partisan lines or hinges on a caucus position, the patterns of support and opposition change with almost every vote. One legislator stated that he and his wife agree on issues only 50 percent of the time, so he felt that agreeing with a certain lobbying group even 25 percent of the time is good. For example, a legislator may not be willing to vote for library districts because his or her constituents would consider the change a potential tax increase. That same legislator may, however, be willing to help defeat a pornography bill or pass a patron privacy bill. Libraries are the focus of many governmental decisions, whether local, state, or federal, and the library lobbyist needs to maintain the goodwill of every decision maker. A positive vote carries just as much weight on the next issue as it does on the first.

TALK TO ALL LEGISLATORS

When time is short, it is tempting to talk to only enough decision makers to get a simple majority vote in favor of a library issue. But remember the advice above about possibly needing a decision maker's vote at some point in the future. Make sure that a decision maker is not ignored just because his or her vote is not immediately necessary for successful passage of the library issue.

In addition, a lobbyist cannot always tell who, if anyone, holds a power vote on a particular issue. If an individual has expertise in certain areas as a result of his or her background or experience, other decision makers will consistently look to that person for guidance in those areas. A lobbyist may not be able to predict where these individual power pockets are or will appear, although occasionally they are obvious. For example, I am persuasive on library issues because of my past experience and expertise. The same holds true in some area for most decision makers. Although power areas exist, not all bills lend themselves to a single issue that one person can affect. Lobbyists cannot therefore rely on providing information only to the person they believe will be most persuasive on a bill. They must communicate with all of the decision makers. Informing all decision makers pays off greatly in the long run. The information the librarian-lobbyist provides to them will be reinforced by the decision maker or makers holding the power votes. Besides, favoritism is obvious and not appreciated.

Conversely, if an obviously powerful decision maker is not contacted ahead of time about an issue or asked to sponsor a bill or ordinance concerning an issue strongly associated with him or her, other decision makers will notice. If this person is offended and speaks against the measure, a bill may be killed simply because of failure to communicate with the right person.

One of the first responsibilities of a library lobbyist is to determine which decision makers could have an effect, positive or adverse, on a particular library issue. The library lobbyist must then make sure that those whose effect would be positive are sponsors, and those whose effect would be adverse are convinced not to speak against the issue. Sometimes the latter situation is the best a library lobbyist can negotiate. Decision makers likely to have a positive effect on library issues include former or current librarians; former school board members; former or current library board members; former or current teachers or university professors; former or current authors or publishers; former or current county commissioners, city council members, aldermen or alderwomen; school superintendents, principals, etc., if the initiative is at a lower level of government; former newspaper reporters or editors; and former or current spouses of any of the above. These people will have had experience with library-related issues, from budgets and freedom of speech to library use. Use those people to your advantage, but do not take them for granted. They may even disagree with you about a library issue.

A final note is that regardless of how powerful your supporters are or how well you have communicated with all of the decision makers, several pitfalls could ruin the best-made plans. First, a party caucus can remove the power person's ability to persuade other decision makers. If a library issue becomes partisan and your supporters are in the wrong party, they lose their power position. Second, a bill will occasionally fail for no apparent reason other than that the legislative body is in a bad mood. Sometimes a bill will fail because the vote is too late in the day or the bill is introduced at an odd time. The Wyoming senate has a "2:30 rule" whereby almost every bill voted on at 2:30 in the afternoon is killed—not purposefully, but consistently. Third, a legislative body may want to give one of its members a victory, even if it means defeating a good bill. If a legislator is having a bad day and loses every issue, without discussion, the body may "give him one." Finally, sometimes apathy stands in the way of passing a good bill. No legislators may be against a bill for any specific reason, but if they do not have a very good reason to vote for it, a good bill may die for lack of interest. Organized lobbying by local constituents and lobbying every decision maker individually helps avoid these pitfalls to some extent, but they often loom up unexpectedly, and they are hard to fight.

RESPOND QUICKLY TO LEGISLATIVE REQUESTS

Although sometimes it takes years to pass a bill, and weeks before a bill is heard after it is introduced, once a particular bill or ordinance begins moving through the process, it often moves so rapidly that even a lobbyist on site has a hard time keeping abreast of all the problems. It is during this time that legislators and decision makers make frantic calls requesting the information that you sent them a few weeks earlier, or updated information, or compiled information, or a shorter version of the information they already have, etc. When a decision maker requests information from you, the first question should be, "When do you need this?" The answer will most likely be "yesterday," but accommodate the decision maker as well and as rapidly as you can. The good library lobbyist will work nonstop on a request until the information is in the decision maker's hands. The librarian may have to work all night, telephone all over the state or country, and then fax like mad, but the results are worth the effort. You will increase your credibility, and when the decision maker can answer factually the questions asked in debate or in committee, his or her credibility on the bill is also enhanced.

Information is not only critical in persuading other decision makers to vote a certain way; it is also necessary to counter arguments, both legitimate and off-base. A certain poetic license exists among legislating bodies that allows a decision maker to occasionally ad lib with intelligent guesses and then substantiate the argument later. Therefore, if a decision maker speaks erroneously against a bill or ordinance and the library sponsor cannot come up with countering facts fast, the wrong information may be the most legitimate-sounding argument regardless of merit or veracity. Generally, we hope the truth prevails, and that the decision maker with the best facts wins unless there is simple philosophical disagreement or the bill meets one of the common pitfalls discussed above. Nevertheless, the library lobbyist should be ready to respond immediately to a decision maker's request for more information.

RESPECT A DECISION MAKER'S RIGHT
TO DISAGREE AND CHALLENGE YOU

A library lobbyist should not feel threatened when a decision maker disagrees with the proposed library legislation. Decision makers tell dozens of lobbyists, individuals, and groups every year that they do not and will not support the legislation sponsored or advocated by that group. The decision maker states his or her position factually to the lobbyist with the understanding that the lobbyist recognizes that unanimous support of any bill is rare. In fact, it is good to know ahead of time which decision makers will not support a library bill so that their constituents can contact that decision maker. It is also good to know, if possible, which legislators will actively fight a library bill and what their arguments are. If you ask a decision maker if he or she can support your bill and the decision maker says "no," gently try to determine what his or her arguments are against it. You might be able to obtain countering information prior to the floor debate or in-chambers argument in order to prime your own sponsors and supporters. A good sponsor will sometimes help you out in this area, since a principal role of a sponsor is to lobby fellow decision makers. Nevertheless, take a "no support" conversation graciously. Do not feel personally offended by nonsupportive decision makers.

COMMUNICATE WITH DECISION MAKERS AS YOUR
BILL PASSES THROUGH THE LEGISLATIVE PROCESS

Most legislatures have a committee system. Once a bill has been assigned to a committee and the committee is "working the bill," the legislators who are not on the committee will be unaware of any changes until the bill passes out of committee and the legislative body as a whole is informed about the committee amendments. It is a good idea to prepare new information about the bill when it comes out of committee to give to all legislators. This new information should outline the committee changes and exlain which changes the library supports and which ones it opposes. Although this tip lends itself most readily to state legislatures, some city councils or county supervisors may have a committee system as well.

Library lobbyists should be aware of a procedural trick here. A committee's amendments will usually be presented to the floor of the house, assembly, or senate for adoption. If a committee changes the bill and the library world does not agree with the changes, defeating the standing committee amendments takes fewer votes than amending the bill back to its original state after the committee of the whole has adopted it. For example, say a legislative body consists of thirty members and is voting on whether or not to adopt a standing committee's amendments. It takes only fifteen votes to defeat adoption of the amendments (a tie vote fails). If the decision-making body adopts those amendments and an individual legislator tries to delete the changes by amending the bill later, he or she must find sixteen votes to pass the amendment. Therefore, if changes are made in committee with which the library world disagrees, the time to challenge the changes is when the bill comes out of the standing committee.

The library lobbyist should therefore contact all legislators about changes as the bill progresses and the status of the bill in process. The library sponsor may have suggestions regarding timing of such notification. As mentioned earlier, one group in Wyoming effectively contacted legislators every day as its bill went through its first, second, and third reading. Even though all the legislators knew the status of the bill because it was before them, the short personal note on each legislator's desk each day served as a reminder of the importance of the bill as well as provided a little humor in a sometimes humorless day. The "poetic" note legislators received on the final reading of the bill was:

> For the last four days we've sent in notes
> of assorted sayings and thought-out quotes.
> Today is third reading and our goal is in sight,
> *Please Vote Yes on the Victim's Bill of Rights!*

The vote was almost unanimous on this bill.

HAVE A SENSE OF HUMOR AND USE IT

As shown above, a little humor, even on an extremely serious issue, can help gain support for a bill. Humor will not usually disguise a bad idea or cover up flaws, but it will make decision makers feel good about voting for a piece of legislation. It also leaves decision makers feeling good about libraries after the bill is gone. Remember, the library continues to have needs that only governments can grant. If the decision makers get a "warm, fuzzy feeling" about a bill or issue whenever it is introduced, you are already ahead. Don't be cutesy, but be clever and humorous in presentation and lobbying. The comic relief will pay off.

Other Do's of Lobbying

It is impossible to cover all the do's of every aspect of lobbying. Some aspects of lobbying lend themselves more readily to rules than others, and this section will cover those areas.

Do's of Legislation

BE AWARE OF PROPOSED LEGISLATION
AFFECTING LIBRARIES

Many public libraries receive copies of bills when they are introduced at the state level.[6] If libraries do not receive copies of pending city ordinances or county resolutions or whatever, the librarian should request that the library be included on the mailing list. Part of the rationale for having copies of all of these proposed changes in law is to provide information to the public. The other specific use of these materials is to keep librarians informed about proposed changes in laws that might affect libraries.[7] Librarians should be aware of bills when they still have an opportunity to provide input to their decision makers.

DEVELOP THOUGHTFUL LIBRARY LEGISLATION

Library legislation can be initiated by one librarian, by a group of librarians, by a committee of librarians, by a legislator—the list goes on and on. At the state level, often a legislative committee of the state library association may be the initiator. Once one of these initiating entities decides on a concept that requires a change in law, the next step is for that entity to determine how to draft the legislation and how to obtain statewide or district-wide support of the concept. The "how-to" will vary depending on whether the issue can be resolved locally or whether a statewide effort is necessary to make the change.

At the state level, an agency usually exists whose primary purpose is to help legislators and legislative committees draft bills. Although the individuals working in this branch can do the actual drafting of the bill, they need to know specifically what the sponsor wants and needs before they can draft appropriate legislation. At the local level, drafting legislation varies widely because of the wide array of governance structures. Librarians need to determine whether the legislative concept they support has statewide implications or whether it is something that can be resolved locally. After that, they need to determine how drafting is done and who does it.

Next, the librarian or librarians with the legislative concept should contact other librarians they think might have a similar need. It is important to solicit the help of decision makers early on as well. Decision makers can make suggestions, troubleshoot, and serve as a liaison between the governing body and the librarians.

Once the library lobbyist has convened an interested group and determined the process for drafting a bill, the work begins. The group should be representative of all parts of the state if it is a state concern, or consist of librarians from all parts of the city, county, school district, or university if it is a local concern. Everyone should have significant input and everyone's concerns should be addressed.[8] Librarians may want to keep the work confidential until they agree upon the final rough draft, at which time the committee should send copies to interested parties and ask for comments and suggestions. The final rough draft should include a fiscal impact statement if possible since a governing body usually asks fiscal questions first.[9]

The initiating committee needs to review carefully the questions and input it receives from librarians in response to its request for input. The more people who are included initially and who feel they had significant input, the better the subsequent support at the grass roots.

After the organizing group incorporates suggestions and finishes its work, it should deliver the draft to the agreed-upon sponsor or sponsors. The decision maker will contact the appropriate bill-drafting service for the governing body. As discussed previously, this agency will conform the proposed bill to the language in the rest of the statutes or ordinances, see that the bill is put in the right section of the statutes, and make sure that the bill indeed says what it is supposed to and is not ambiguous.

Without appropriate expertise or experience on the committee, the initiating group may only be able to decide on a concept and not be able to create a rough draft of a bill. A concept is usually sufficient. At the state level a legislator often just gives the drafting service an idea, such as, "Draft a bill for me on state aid to public libraries. Pattern it after the one in California." Be careful here, however, because such a bill may not reflect the library committee's vision unless it gives the bill drafter more specific instructions. At the very minimum, the group involved in developing the original idea for the proposed change in law should prepare a list of key features it wants included in the legislation.

DO'S OF TESTIFYING FOR OR AGAINST PROPOSED LEGISLATION

Once the bill is drafted and introduced to the appropriate standing committee or governing body, a librarian-lobbyist should testify on behalf of the legislation if possible. If the librarian opposes a bill, he or she should attempt to testify against it. For the most part the do's of testifying are appropriate in both situations.

When a bill is heard for the first time before a committee, the city council, school board, etc., the sponsor or the library lobbyist must give a thorough presentation to that group. Although every member of the committee or board previously received a copy of the proposed legislation and theoretically read it, the bill still must be explained to the committee or board. Often a sponsor will allow the primary proponent of the bill to present the detailed explanation to the committee, for several reasons. First, a presentation by the proponent gives the sponsor a chance once again to listen carefully to the proponent's explanation so that the sponsor will be ready when it is his or her responsibility to explain it on the floor or to the whole governing body. Second, the librarian who drafted the bill or worked with a committee to draft a bill knows the issue best and can answer the questions most knowledgeably. Finally, a committee may be impressed with a sincere and concerned librarian. Protocol may require a legislator to make the presentation, with supporting testimony from the bill's proponents.

It is important to plan your scheduled time allotment carefully prior to the hearing. The librarian or legislator responsible for the primary explanation of the bill should summarize briefly for the committee what the need for the legislation is and what the bill does. Then the librarian-lobbyist or legislator should present it in an orderly section-by-section summary.[10] The library should also prepare a written summary of each section of a complicated bill to give to the committee. If the librarian-lobbyist wants the committee to amend the bill, he or she should prepare the proposed amendment ahead of time. The proposed amendment or amendments should be typed and distributed to each member after the initial presentation or whenever the committee chair indicates it is an appropriate time to entertain amendments.[11] The librarian-lobbyist should actually "plug" extensive changes into the text of a clean bill and make copies to distribute to committee members.

When more than one person plans to testify, the committee chair, the mayor, the school board president, etc., should know about it before the presentation if possible. There may be insufficient time for all presenters, and the committee chair may ask the library group to limit the number of people who speak. These individuals should make their presentations in an orderly and brief succession.[12] They should not exceed their allotted time, although the governing group may ask them to stay longer to answer questions.

Make sure that in addition to the sponsors of the bill, many additional supporters are at the hearing, even if they do not say anything.[13] Decision makers sometimes listen more carefully when the hearing room is packed with supporters. A large group attending also shows decision makers that many individuals are interested in the bill under consideration, not just the sponsor or the primary speakers. Often the opposition shows up as well, so it is essential to have a good showing of supporters. I have experienced a room packed with nutritionists fighting chiropractors, defense attorneys fighting plaintiff attorneys, and a large group of hearing-impaired individuals crammed into the committee room with their signer as they "listened" to debate on telephone service for the hearing impaired. It makes a difference to decision makers to know that supporters are interested enough to show up simply to hear the testimony on a particular bill.

If it appears the committee is positive and seems willing to vote favorably on the bill, cut your presentation short, even if some supporters still waiting to testify had to travel a long distance to be present. It is better to go with the flow than to stick by your original schedule.

Don'ts of Lobbying Etiquette

Universal Basics

As with the do's of lobbying etiquette, some actions are universally ineffective and should be avoided. The purpose of lobbying is not only to get what you want immediately but also to lay groundwork so that you can get what you want in the future as well. Avoiding some of the don'ts will help prevent librarian-lobbyists from getting into a position where they will not only lose their bill of today but will also lose their credibility for efforts of tomorrow.

What the Experts Say

The top three don'ts that legislators and lobbyists listed in Jacklyn Ducote's survey are presented below.

1. Don't lie, withhold information, or misrepresent the opposition. Twenty-nine legislators and forty-nine lobbyists
   mentioned these.
2. Don't threaten or get personal. Seventeen legislators and
   nineteen lobbyists stated these were important.
3. Don't be pushy, arrogant, argumentative, sarcastic, or ha-
   rassing. Twenty-three legislators and nine lobbyists included these in their recommendations.

Note that about the same number of legislators mentioned number 3 as mentioned number 1, yet only 9 lobbyists mentioned number 3, forty fewer than mentioned number 1. The reason for this
discrepancy may be that legislators are on the receiving end of the
sarcastic, nagging, overbearing, and arrogant lobbyists, and often
lobbyists do not even realize how they come across!

A discussion of each of the above will illustrate exactly what
can happen if the librarian-lobbyist does the wrong thing. The first
don't is the converse of the do regarding telling the truth. Omitting
information falls somewhere between lying and telling the truth.
The bottom line is to maintain credibility and establish a reputation
of reliability with your decision makers. One small lie or misrep-
resentation can ruin a relationship and destroy the trust that has
taken you months or even years to build. The best lobbyists tell
the truth, regardless of whether it hurts the lobbyist's cause. Decision makers talk among themselves, and news about an untruthful
lobbyist travels fast. One little lie may sprout into a whole tree of
distrust. Lying is simply not worth the risk of losing your credibility
and good relationship with legislators.

Misrepresenting the opposition is another issue of great importance to decision makers. A decision maker will more likely sponsor
a piece of legislation if he or she is assured that it is a noncontroversial bill and that there is no known opposition. Obviously, one
can never anticipate all opposition prior to introduction of a bill.
Nevertheless, if there is established opposition, even if it is internal
within the library world, it is essential to communicate this to the
sponsor and other decision makers whose support you seek. Possible controversy is one additional factor that decision makers must
consider when getting involved in an issue. Often, a decision maker
wants to contact the other group to get its side of the story. The effective library lobbyist will already have prepared information on
the opposition's arguments to present to the decision maker. The
presentation should accurately reflect the opposition's arguments,

and the library lobbyist should have answers to the opposition's stance, to the extent possible. If you have gained credibility with the decision makers, they may research no further and simply use your information to make a decision. They will appreciate your providing them information on the pros and cons.

The second most often mentioned don't is not to threaten or get personal.[14] A decision maker is a public servant and attempts to make the best decisions possible in order to represent the will of his or her constituency whenever that can be determined. It is hard work, and a vast majority of interactions decision makers have with individuals do not involve thanking the decision makers for their fine efforts. Most interactions involve people with problems, angry people, or people demanding or needing something. Obviously most decision makers would not be in politics if they wanted to avoid that kind of interaction. On the other hand, there is a difference between threatening or making personal slurs and simply being angry about a situation. Threatening a decision maker is ineffective and unpersuasive. It may make the lobbyist feel better, but it will not effect a change. A decision maker sees himself or herself as a problem solver. Like all human beings, when decision makers are attacked, the hair on the back of their neck stands up and they are ready to fight! Threats or personal derogatory remarks give the lobbyist and the library a bad name.

Finally, a lobbyist must avoid pushiness, arrogance, or any of the other nasty habits legislators named as being negative. "Who me, arrogant?" Arrogance is a pitfall of many bright, well-informed, articulate individuals. As I have pointed out several times, decision makers are, by the nature of the task given them, ignorant individuals. There is too much to know, too much to read, and too many issues for a decision maker to be able to have a good working knowledge of all of them. Consequently, decision makers often look dumb, ask dumb questions, and act dumb. They are not dumb, however. They simply do not have the same background that a librarian or any other special interest person does. They do not understand all the acronyms that librarians whip around so easily, such as OCLC, CARL, NCLIS, etc. Many of them never learned their way around a card catalog, much less a computerized database. So when they ask dumb questions, a library lobbyist cannot be impatient, because the impatience comes across as arrogance. A library lobbyist cannot say, "As I have told you many times before . . . " because such a comment is condescending. A library lobbyist cannot say, "If you'd read your material, you'd know . . . "

because such a comment is overbearing. Treat decision makers the way the best teachers treat students. Students do not always catch on right away, and some students need to hear something many times before remembering it. Lobbying is a teaching process and when the lobbyist gets frustrated because he or she believes the decision maker should already know something, then it is time for the library lobbyist to take control of his or her emotions and be kind to the seemingly dumb decision maker.

Other Recommended Don'ts

In addition to the top three don'ts discussed above, legislators (including me), lobbyists, and authors on lobbying recommend avoiding a variety of additional behaviors when attempting to interact persuasively with decision makers at all levels.[15]

DON'T SCOLD OFFICIALS

Scolding is yet another form of being overbearing or condescending. It may initiate an unnecessary power struggle without changing anyone's mind or vote. It is always tempting to let someone know what you really think. However, in the long run scolding only alienates a decision maker and gets the library lobbyist no closer to the library's goal.

DON'T DEMAND SUPPORT

"Mother's rules" come in handy in good lobbying. Saying "please" instead of "gimme" works not only on parents but also on legislators. Stamping your foot, crossing your arms, looking disgusted, or writing forcefully will not intimidate a decision maker into changing his or her position on an issue. Good solid information, impeccable reasoning, and the likelihood of success are all much more effective in persuading a legislator to vote in favor of a bill.

DON'T OFFER INCENTIVES FOR A VOTE, SUCH AS
MONEY, GIFTS, AND PROMISES OF POLITICAL SUPPORT

In recent years legislators all over the United States have resigned when news of proposed bribes and shady dealings was released. If you make an offer of money, gifts, or promises of political support to one of the majority of decision makers who do not take kindly to such offers, you will embarrass yourself and lose your credibility. Such an offer is not worth the risk to the library's reputation and your own.

Don't make campaign contributions on the heels of or prior to a critical vote. Even if such a donation is unrelated to the vote, if it looks as though there is a connection and takes on the appearance of impropriety, you will lose. If you want to contribute to a decision maker's war chest, do so during campaign season.

DON'T MAKE A PROMISE YOU CAN'T KEEP

It is easy to forget to do something when asked, even if the request came from a decision maker. Librarians are often overworked, and many library activists lobby in their spare time. As noted previously, if you are asked to do something for a decision maker and you agree to do it, treat the task as an urgent reference question. Answer the question and get back to the patron. This is a task at which librarians should excel. Take advantage of your training and follow through on promises. What do you lose if you do not? Credibility—the key to ongoing lobbying success.

DON'T BE RIGID OR AFRAID TO LOOK
AT ALTERNATIVES

A decision maker is trying to get information from you when discussing your proposal with you. Supportive decision makers often act as devil's advocate because they must anticipate all the questions they might get as proponents or sponsors of the legislation. Nonsupportive decision makers may often ask tough questions because they want to discredit a bill or ordinance. In either case, listen to what the decision maker asks and what the decision maker recommends. They know the system better than you do, and they may have some valid suggestions. Sometimes questioning will lead to an alternative that neither you nor the decision maker anticipated. Do not rule out all options but the one you originally presented.

A LEGISLATOR'S TIME IS LIMITED—DON'T
WASTE IT

Think about how busy you are. A decision maker is just as busy if not busier. A decision maker needs to know only what it is you want and why. Unless the decision maker keeps you longer than you planned, try to keep phone calls to one minute or less, visits to 15 minutes or less, and letters to one page or less.

DON'T TALK TO MALE DECISION MAKERS
MORE THAN FEMALE DECISION MAKERS

Even though there are fewer female than male decision makers and more males serving as committee chairs and on powerful committees, the female decision makers should not be ignored—especially for support of library issues. Librarianship has traditionally been a female profession and it remains so today. Although research is scant, women may be generally more familiar with library issues than men because they typically rely more on libraries to meet their informational needs than men do.[16] Women's votes count as much as men's do, and a woman may very well be the power decision maker within a governing body.

DON'T INTERRUPT DECISION MAKERS
IN THE MIDDLE OF MEALS

Although it may sound elementary, if you see a decision maker eating at a restaurant, as many of them have to do during legislative sessions away from their district, do not "grab the opportunity" to lobby during the meal. Legislators especially have very little time alone during a legislative session. Many have no choice but to eat in public, and they need to have their privacy because that may be about the only time they have to spend with family members or with other legislators one on one. It is terribly inappropriate to interrupt. Don't be surprised if you are greeted very coldly if you try some ad hoc lobbying during mealtimes.

DON'T GIVE GREATER RECOGNITION TO ONE
LEGISLATOR OVER ANOTHER EXCEPT IN THE
CASE OF SPONSORS OR KEY PLAYERS

Again, although it may sound silly, if a lobbyist group decides to recognize supportive decision makers publicly, all of them must be recognized equally, except for sponsors or key players who were directly responsible for the successful passage of your library bill. It is appropriate to quote in a newspaper article or a letter to the editor decision makers who urged other legislators to pass your bill, without listing all of those who voted in favor of the bill. It is not appropriate, however, to list some of those who voted in favor of it without printing the names of all of those who voted for it. Sponsors and key players should get special recognition, but all other supporters who helped pass your legislation should be treated equally.

Other types of recognition may also cause problems. For example, if you decide to send flowers to all council members who voted in favor of your budget, make sure the bouquets are all the same size. In Wyoming, over the years, one lobbyist has consistently sent one female legislator a big bouquet of flowers while all the other female legislators got a rose in a bowl. Decision makers notice such things. Favoritism can backfire, and instead of making a good impression with a gift, a lobbyist can make a bad impression by being selectively generous!

DON'T INVOLVE GRASS ROOTS UNNECESSARILY

It is tempting for any lobbying group to "sic" constituents on a decision maker. It is terribly ineffective, however, if the group unleashes a big group of constituents prematurely or with misinformation. By the time the decision maker gets the tenth urgent phone call with the same mistaken message, whatever effectiveness a calling tree may have had is lost. Decision makers do not have time to defend themselves against misinformed, angry constituents. A deluge of misinformed grass roots messages kills the goodwill that the decision maker had toward an organization, and it makes a decision maker doubt the effectiveness of the group as a whole. This kind of mistake often happens when someone is listening to debate or listening to a committee's questions and misunderstands why a decision maker asks a question or makes a comment. If the librarian-lobbyist determines that a calling tree should be activated, that person must be very sure that he or she knows the decision maker's position and name and accurately communicates that information to the grass roots callers.

In addition, you don't want to wear out your grass roots support. Many people find it difficult to contact a decision maker but are willing to do it for a good cause—once! Don't waste your one shot with unnecessary issues.

Letters Decision Makers Never Finish Reading

Letter writing is a primary way to communicate with decision makers, but obviously it is only effective if the decision maker actually reads the letter. The higher the level of government, the less likely it is for a decision maker to read all letters personally (i.e., congressional aides most often take care of the average letter from a constituent). Nevertheless, the good library lobbyist should attempt to make a letter "readworthy" by starting it with a catchy sentence or one that will grab the reader's attention. Opening sentences that turn the decision maker off mean that the letter may not be read at all. Plan those opening sentences well.

Never begin letters with the kinds of openers listed below.

1. *"Dear Sir:"* The decision maker may be a woman. Such a salutation is probably inappropriate in any case nowadays. The way to address a representative is as follows:[17]

   To Your Senator

   > The Honorable _____ Full Name _____
   > United States Senate
   > Washington, D.C. 20510
   >
   > Dear Senator _____ Last Name _____ :

   To Your Representative

   > The Honorable _____ Full Name _____
   > U. S. House of Representatives
   > Washington, D.C. 20515
   >
   > Dear Representative _____ Last Name _____ :

   To Your State Senator

   > The Honorable _____ Full Name _____
   > Senate Office Building or Senate Chambers
   > State Capitol Building
   > State Capitol, State Zip
   >
   > Dear Senator _____ Last Name _____ :

   To Your State Representative

   > The Honorable _____ Full Name _____
   > House Office Building or House Chambers
   > State Capitol Building
   > State Capitol, State Zip
   >
   > Dear Representative _____ Last Name _____ :

   To Your Local City Council, Mayor, Etc.

   > The Honorable _____ Full Name _____
   > City Council Chambers, City Hall
   > Commissioners' Room, County Courthouse
   > School Administration Buildings, Address
   > University Trustee Hangout
   >
   > Dear Mayor (Commissioner, Alderman) _Last Name_ :

2. *"Dear Senator (wrong name)"*: One organization sent me letters and newsletters with the wrong name on them for

six months. The name was a combination of my first name and another senator's last name. Even though I specifically wrote them to point out the mistake, they did not correct it.

When a decision maker and spouse have different names, it is important to know both names when you address a letter to them.

3. *"Dear Representative Schmich*:   I am disappointed in you." You may be, but don't start a letter out in this fashion unless you are not interested in being effective or attempting to change a decision maker's mind. A sentence like this makes a decision maker defensive, and he or she will read the rest of the letter with a jaundiced or negative point of view, if he or she reads it all.

4. *"Dear Representative Perkins*:   I am a voting taxpayer and if you don't support House Bill 000, I'll personally make sure you never get elected again." Threats do not change decision makers' minds or make them vote or act differently in any way. Certainly many decision makers keep their eye on the next election and want to be reelected, but threatening them with a reelection fight is a poor persuasive technique because it implies that they vote for or against an issue on the basis of personal gain and not on the merits of the bill and the extent to which it represents the interests of their constituency.

5. *"Dear Representative Gardzelewski*:   You're a murderer . . . " Although many might not believe that someone would really begin a letter like this, legislators receive similar letters about everything from environmental issues to animal rights and abortion issues. This is definitely not a good way to start a letter.

6. *"Dear Council Member Huber*:   Please vote against Ordinance #13 . . . " This opening is inappropriate when Huber is a sponsor or a nonsupporter. A lot of people with home computers input a list of decision makers' names and addresses and print form letters for each name on the list. This practice is fine, except in the cases noted above. You do not want to send this kind of a letter to a sponsor of the bill, nor do you need to waste your time or a nonsupporter's time by sending him or her your letter. A letter like this to the wrong person shows the writer's lack of knowledge.

7. *"Dear Alderman Lang*:   Please consider withdrawing your ordinance on junk cars." Although this letter acknowledges

that the writer knows that Alderman Lang is the sponsor and asks him in a polite way to withdraw the bill, it is ineffective. Sometimes a decision maker will sponsor a bill or ordinance that he or she does not support 100 percent. Even so, it is unlikely that a decision maker will withdraw a bill, because he or she has gone out on a limb by sponsoring it initially and will see it through despite criticism. Certainly it is appropriate in some cases for a decision maker to withdraw his or her own bill. Examples are: (1) if the bill was based on erroneous information; (2) if the problem can be solved more easily through other means, and the legislation triggered action that could solve it; (3) if the problem solved itself during the legislative process; or (4) if the initiating group decided against the measure. Before a library lobbyist takes such a drastic measure as requesting the withdrawal of a bill, however, it is important to check the laws and rules of the governing body involved to see when withdrawal may be too late. The bill may have to be "killed" instead of withdrawn; the library lobbyist should know the difference.

Even if letters avoid the off-putting openers discussed above, they may not get read if they fall into either of the following categories.

1. Unsigned letters, letters with a fictitious name, or letters with no return address. These are the most despicable types of letters a decision maker can receive. Usually when a person is unwilling to sign a letter it is because the letter is a mean-spirited personal attack on the decision maker or the decision maker's position on an issue. Avoid the temptation to write such a letter. It is totally ineffective in changing the decision maker's mind, and if the letter addresses a specific issue, the decision maker's opinion of that issue may lower.

2. Letters that are unclear in their message or contents. When a communication is totally unclear on its face and appears to be something it is not (a petition of concerned citizens looking more like a chain letter), the decision maker may toss it upon opening it. A letter should always state clearly in the first sentence or two what its purpose is or it may never be read by its intended audience.

To summarize, letters are a major way that lobbyists and lay lobbyists communicate with their decision makers. The people writing the letters should have a clear purpose in mind. The underlying purpose of every letter to a decision maker is to have a specific impact on the decision maker. Don't approach a legislator in a way that stops the decision maker from even reading your correspondence. Letters should be thoughtfully written and should avoid the above don'ts. Every communication with a decision maker should make a difference and not be simply a waste of paper, ink, and postage.

Notes

1. Elizabeth A. Curry and Susan Sellers Whittle, eds., *Florida Public Library Board Manual* (Tallahassee: Florida Department of State, State Library of Florida, 1988), 75–76; Betty Bay, ed., *Trustee Tool Kit for Library Leadership* (Sacramento: California Association of Library Trustees and Commissioners, California State Library, 1987), 200; Jacklyn H. Ducote, *Winning Ways for Lobbyists: HOT TIPS From Both Sides of the Rail*, "Part 2, Do's for Lobbyists," "Part 3, Don'ts for Lobbyists," 1989; Dorothy Smith, *In Our Own Interest: A Handbook for the Citizen Lobbyist in State Legislatures* (Seattle: Madrona Publishers, Inc., 1979); and Georgia Robertson, ed., *Nebraska Trustees Handbook* (The Nebraska Library Commission and The Trustees, Users and Friends Section of the Nebraska Library Association, 1990), 124–25.

2. Jacklyn H. Ducote, *Winning Ways for Lobbyists*, "Part 1, Overview, Survey Results."

3. Ducote, "Part 2. Do's for Lobbyists."

4. See note 1 above for just a few of the many excellent trustee handbooks available. Check with your state library association or state library to determine if they have published a handbook geared toward the needs in your state.

5. Notably the *Nebraska Trustees Handbook* and Ducote, Part 2.

6. Steve Sherman, "Support Your Local VIP's," *ABC's of Library Promotion*, 2nd ed. (Metuchen, N. J.: The Scarecrow Press, 1980), 162.

7. Ibid.

8. Dorothy Smith, *In Our Own Interest: A Handbook for the Citizen Lobbyist in State Legislatures*, 30.

9. Ibid.

10. Ibid., 99.

11. Ibid.

12. Ibid.

13. Ibid.

14. Ducote, "Part 3, Don'ts for Lobbyists." See also *Florida Public Library Board Manual*, 76; and *Trustee Tool Kit for Library Leadership*, 200.

15. See expecially *Florida Public Library Board Manual*, Ducote, Part 3, and *Trustee Tool Kit for Library Leadership*, from which many of these specific don'ts are drawn.

16. Bernard Vavrek, *Assessing the Information Needs of Rural Pennsylvanians* (Clarion, Pa.: College of Library Science, Clarion University of Pennsylvania, 1990), 24.

17. Curry and Whittle, eds., *Florida Public Library Board Manual*, 77.

7

Lobbying for Public Libraries

Typical Funding Sources

Most public libraries are part of a government and consequently look to government for their funding. Public libraries generally receive funds or services from all three levels of government. Although percentages differ, the generally agreed-upon percentage of funding for public libraries is 82 to 91 percent local funding, 7 to 12 percent state funding, and 2 to 5 percent federal funding.[1]

Because this funding is typically a function of the political process, it is neither constant nor predictable.[2] Consequently, public libraries face the major task of lobbying for funding.

Much of the emphasis of lobbying nationwide is on federal and state funding. However, some librarians have realized that because the majority of funds available are local and are appropriated by local officials, they should spend a majority of their time lobbying at the local level.[3] Even so, state statutes and the governance of the library affect the total amount of money available to public libraries.

Table 5   Typical Sources—Local, State, and Federal Library Funding*

Local Source (Funding for *individual local* libraries, city, county special district libraries)	State Source (Includes funding for *cooperative library systems* for special statewide library programs or individual local libraries.)	Federal Source (Supplementary funding for cooperative library systems and individual public libraries.)
1. Dedicated library tax derived from property taxes.	1. *State Library Services Acts*	1. *Library Services and Construction Act (LSCA)* Grants administered by state libraries.
2. Allocation from the city or county General Fund (made up of sales tax, property tax, etc.)	a. Encourages and enables *sharing and coordination* of library resources among and between libraries.	2. Examples of other *federal program* grants used by libraries:
3. Special district library and county library funding is from a fixed property tax proration.	b. Subsidizes direct loans and interlibrary loans by and for residents of other libraries.	a. HUD—Community Development Block grants.
4. Special districts and county libraries may also receive Special District Augmentation Funds from the county in some states.	c. Often similar in construction to LSCA.	b. National Endowment for the Humanities.
5. Special Tax Propositions.	2. *Public Library Finance Act (PLF)*	
6. Library revenues—fines, fees, booksales, bequests, etc.	a. Supplementary funding for local public libraries.	
7. Special grants—Foundations, local community grants, service clubs, etc.	b. Provides state match for local operating budget.	
	3. *State Aid to Public Libraries*	
	a. Attempt to decrease funding disparity between libraries or library districts.	
	b. Can be based on per capita distribution, grant per county, or grant per library or library system.	
	4. *State Humanities Councils*	
	5. *State Arts Councils*	

*Adapted from *Trustee Tool Kit for Library Leadership*, Betty Bay, ed.

Some state statutes limit library funding to a specific number of tax mills dedicated for funding the public library system, or they limit the total number of mills a taxing district can levy. Often the taxing district will include libraries as one of many services that are funded by the mills. Therefore, if one budget within the limited mill levy is increased, another must be cut. Hence, the age-old battle between public library funding and funding for police protection or health services. If the library is funded by a special library district, a cap on the taxing amount may exist. Consequently, regardless of local support, the state legislature will set the parameters of how supportive the local government can be in terms of tax dollars.

Governance also affects funding and is often established by statute by the state legislature. Five typical governance structures for libraries exist: (1) the library is part of a city or county government and has no board of trustees or only an advisory board; (2) the library is a department of a city or county government and has a policy-making board as well; (3) the library operates as an independent not-for-profit corporation, with or without independent taxing authority; (4) the library is part of state government, and (5) the library is part of a system of libraries.[4] The power of each of these kinds of boards varies with its role within the governmental structure. I suggest that a first step in any lobbying effort is to determine the legal parameters of public library funding and governance. If the library is not receiving the full amount of local funding it could receive under the state statutes, the focus of first lobbying efforts should be local. If the library is receiving all possible funding under the statutory scheme, it may be time to approach state legislators for a change in the state funding scheme.

Taxes Mean Lobbying!

Funds for the operating budgets of the majority of public libraries come primarily from revenues generated by cities or counties, whose funding base is taxes. The main type of tax allocated to libraries is local property (*ad valorem*) tax that the city or county appropriates annually. Some cities or counties fund library services by implementing state legislation that allows a local option of an additional penny sales tax for different purposes, such as construction or even maintenance of local government services. Depending on the way such legislation is worded, libraries can be included on the ballot as a specific project recipient on which the voters decide. Other types of taxes that have funded libraries in past years include the timber yield tax, transit-lodging tax, and dedicated-purpose library tax.[5] Some libraries are even funded from the city or county general fund. General fund monies usually come from taxes, so again, the primary source of funding for even these libraries is taxes.[6]

The best and most thorough discussion of campaigning for library ballot initiatives is found in *Campaigning for Libraries*, published in 1988 by The Central Colorado Library System.[7]

Often, local funding initiatives not connected directly to the library will impact the library considerably. For instance, the Broward County Library Board and Friends worked to pass the extra penny sales tax because its passage meant forty million new tax dollars for the county. Once the county is richer, the library has a greater chance of getting more money. In this case, the resulting increase in the public library budget exceeded the amount that would have been realized from fully funded and authorized state aid.[8] A librarian has limited time and resources and should take into account the ultimate impact his or her efforts will have on the library.

States appropriate money to public libraries from a variety of sources. For example, Ohio funds libraries from state-collected income tax and local property tax.[9] Other states fund public libraries by specific legislative enactment. In California, a regional cooperative library system is funded through the California Library Services Act (CLSA). This legislation sets aside funds for libraries participating in programs specified under the legislation. The Cooperative Library System consists of fifteen regional cooperative library systems that exist as independent local entities through an agreement among its member jurisdictions. The governance of this system is different from that of most citizen boards. Each regional cooperative system is governed by an administrative council composed of head librarians of member libraries. Administrative council members propose a system budget and submit it to a state board which then submits it to the legislature through the state librarian.[10]

Many libraries supplement their budgets through the state library (distributor of federal LSCA funds); through specific state legislation benefiting libraries such as state aid to public libraries or state acts patterned after LSCA principles and purposes[11]; through friend's groups; through individual library foundations established for the purpose of obtaining additional funding for libraries (501c3 nonprofit organizations established by an affiliate of the library, as opposed to private foundations organized by an individual or corporation for a particular purpose not connected to the library in any way); through federal programs (for example, National Endowments for the Humanities and Arts and Community Development Block Grant funds); through state programs (for example, the state council on arts or humanities); through bond issues; through tax levies if the library is in a district which allows them[12]; through individual private foundations not connected to the library, such as the old Carnegie Foundation; through individuals; and so on.

Regardless of how a library's budget is patched together to form a complete budget, librarians need to recognize that the bulk of their funding is nevertheless from taxes and is therefore allocated locally. A major problem seems to be how to maintain the level of funding allocated locally when libraries must compete with welfare, police, public works, health, education, and other fundamental services.[13] As mentioned previously, if the library is not receiving all the funds it could through local sources, perhaps a majority of the librarian's lobbying efforts should be directed toward the local government first.

Librarians should be aware that their share of the state and local tax pie is exceedingly small. In 1982–83, this amount was less than one-half of one percent.[14] Libraries remain underfunded and underrated by the individuals who have the power to make decisions about funding. This is why librarians need to develop a thoughtful and systematic lobbying effort and to get to know well the decision makers in their district, city, and state.

Profile of a Typical Local Decision Maker

Justifying library funding to the appropriate legislative body is often difficult. As mentioned numerous times throughout this book, librarians need to develop relationships with the appropriate individuals *before* a situation arises that requires political assistance. When working with elected officials, librarians must assume that most are competent, committed, and well-meaning individuals.[15] However, a decision maker has many diverse issues to face, and the library is not usually at the top of the list. The librarian must also always assume that the elected official knows very little about libraries. Typically, uninformed decision makers (including city council members, county commissioners, etc.) often believe a library is a library is a library. A major goal of any lobbying effort is to educate the individuals who decide how much funding to allocate to libraries so that they no longer have the age-old misconceptions about what a library is or is not.

This is a frustrating goal because legislative bodies constantly change, and the librarian must educate new individuals when they take office or are appointed. In addition, the job is not through even when a librarian thinks that he or she has worked with a particular decision maker long enough to provide that person with sufficient information to understand the library's issues and specific problems. Successful lobbying on behalf of libraries includes educating and reeducating the *same* individual about libraries on a regular basis. Even though the librarian believes he or she has communicated the library's needs to a decision maker, the librarian must reiterate the library's needs over and over again and in more than one way. A decision maker has to know too much to be able to remember everything.

For example, suppose a library district is working on a building program. Early in the process, the library board members approach the county commissioners to gain their support. After the county commissioners hear the board chairman's plea for a bond issue and receive a thick packet of information on the library's building needs, the board leaves feeling the job is done. Wrong! The job has just begun. If the packet the board gave to the commissioners consists of a great deal of information without a summary sheet, the commissioners may just put the information away until they can find time to look at it closely or give it to an aide to summarize for them. This is especially true when the decision makers are part-time. That is, they are elected to a political position that meets once or twice a month for an evening or a day, but they continue with their jobs as real estate agents, businessmen and businesswomen, or whatever. They receive too much information from all sources to be expected to remember details about any one source.

Let's say that the decision makers know generally about the library's problems and budgetary needs. It is not an insult to any of the decision makers to repeat the library's problems in every subsequent presentation the library makes to the same body. A librarian must assume that at least one of the decision makers has forgotten what the librarian presented previously and that a "refresher course" is necessary. A reminder to decision makers before every major decision affecting the library will bring better results, and the government official will also appreciate being refreshed.

Generally, a library director or a trustee will appear before a funding body annually regarding budget concerns, and as the need arises for discussing a tax increase for a special district; for placing a bond issue on a ballot if a new building is needed; for seeking support of state or federal library funding legislation; or for other dollar-related issues.

As mentioned previously, if a librarian presents written information to a decision-making body for the first time at a meeting, and the decision makers have to listen to the librarian's presentation at the same time they are reading or skimming the information just handed to them, the librarian can be assured that the decision maker will not fully understand either the written information or the oral presentation. The more effective way to present information is to make an oral presentation first and then distribute the written materials. Even better, if the librarian can send the written materials before the meeting, the decision makers will theoretically have time to read and absorb the material and come to the meeting with questions.

Librarians should realize that even if they send material ahead of time, at least one decision maker will not have had the time to read it and will ask a "dumb" question that was answered in the materials the librarian sent. Librarians should never, under any circumstances, begin their answer by commenting, "If you had read the materials I sent you . . . " Answer the question as if it were one of the more brilliant questions that had ever been asked. Additionally, almost without exception, decision makers all listening to a presentation in the same room at the same time will ask the same question at least twice. It is difficult for anyone to absorb a great deal of oral information at one time. People selectively hear different points a librarian makes in his or her presentation.

Even though one decision maker asked a certain question ten minutes ago and the librarian answered it eloquently, when the librarian is asked the same question again by another decision maker, the librarian should answer it exactly the same way he or she did the first time. Again, the librarian should not cut the answer short and should resist saying, "As I mentioned a few minutes ago . . . " Remember that most decision makers are well-meaning and hardworking, but often they have just too much information to absorb at one time.

Typical Budgetary Profile and Problems

Providing Budget Information
to Decision Makers

To a great extent, the ability of a library to serve its community, whether the patrons are school children, the public, or professors, depends upon its funding level. Creative librarians can often work miracles with very little, but a sustained low budget eventually erodes the collection and library services. Funding levels are established by the governing body or bodies of a library. By its very nature, the budgeting process involves making priorities within a set number of defined needs and a more or less anticipated dollar amount. Governing bodies do not make their decisions in a void—they need information as much as any patron who walks in the door of the library. Without sufficient information, a governing body is forced to either allocate to libraries what is left over after funding other needs or make an unscientific guess as to the library's financial needs.

As a result, the politically shy librarian need only equate the needs of the governing body with those of the patrons. Lobbying is not really lobbying at all—it is simply providing information to individuals who may not know they need it! More important, the library's life depends on it. The first and most important part of any lobbying effort is INFORMATION! Since libraries specialize in information, librarians should be, hands down, the best lobbyists around.

What kind of information should a library provide to a governing body? Two kinds—minimal and extensive. As mentioned previously, members of governing bodies have a limited amount of time to read, ponder, and compare. Just as librarians see journals, memos, and mail pile up daily, so do decision makers. The shorter, more concise, and fact-filled summary of its needs that a library can provide to a decision maker, the better. A one-page summary is the best, but three pages may not be too much. The governing body should be able to tell at a glance what the library's needs are, what its income sources are, and what the library is asking of it. If the library's needs are not clear immediately, one or more members may not take the time to track down the information necessary to make an informed decision.

At least two kinds of decision makers exist. One group of decision makers does not read what they receive, or they simply skim the information and wait for a presentation or discussion by the governing body as a whole. The one- to three-page "Executive Summary" mentioned above meets this group's needs.

The second group of decision makers likes to receive massive quantities of information in order to feel comfortable about making a decision. If a question arises, or if a member of a governing board belongs to this second group and actually likes and uses information to his or her advantage, a librarian should not be caught by surprise. The librarian must provide sufficient documentation and information to answer any potential question that might be asked. All executive summaries, therefore, should be backed up with a very detailed justification, and the librarian should submit both to the governing body at the same time.

Often, decisions are made when the librarian is not present. The librarian must therefore provide detailed information that is easy to use and that satisfies the needs of every member of the governing board, regardless of whether they like a lot of or a little information.

Again, this is an area in which librarians should excel—making a large amount of detailed information easy to use and available. Using tabs, indexes, color coding, large print, pictures, and graphs in budget and other presentations allows the decision maker to wade through detailed budget information easily. One librarian gives a poignant example of how effective a graph can be. The mayor had asked all agencies, including the library, to reduce their budgets in a particularly tight year. Notwithstanding the directive, the library board instructed the librarian to ask for an increase. The director presented a pie chart with the library's slice of one-half of one percent of the total revenues projected, which looked like a straight line. She asked, "Where are you going to make a reduction, and, if you do, what difference will it make anyway?" The library got its increase.[16]

What to Include in a Budget

A major question for every budget compiler is, "to pad or not to pad?" A librarian does not want to be accused of being dishonest with the decision makers or of inflating the library's budgetary needs. On the other hand, decision makers rarely, if ever, pass a budget without leaving their mark on it because that is their job. If they simply approved the budgets presented to them, they could be accused of rubber-stamping and not being thorough or prudent enough with taxpayer dollars. One thing a librarian can count on is that every library budget they submit will be changed during the budgeting process by someone.

After years of submitting a "bare bones" budget to the county commissioners who cut it additionally every time, and after watching the legislative process in action for eight years whereby no budget went unchanged, I have come to the conclusion that the librarian and the library board should ask for what the library needs without shame, knowing that their request will be cut nevertheless. Few libraries have everything they need, so this kind of request is naturally padded without being dishonest. Avoid the temptation to say, "They'll never fund this, so let's not ask for it even though we really need it."

A critical issue in submitting such a budget is what kind of veto power the funding body has over the library's budget. Can the county council decide not to fund library books this year or to "redline" a particular position? When the funding body outside the library has the power to cut a specific item in the library's budget, it is called a "line-item veto" power. Librarians should oppose the granting of this power to funding bodies. If they have it already, libraries will want to convince the decision makers, if possible, to delete items in the library's priority order. In other words, let the library decide what the priority list is and then ask the decision makers to cut the bottom of the list first. A better situation is one in which the funding body decides the dollar amount and leaves the cutting to the library.

Another way to approach a budget is to list necessities—what a library absolutely needs in order to function, what the library needs in order to meet today's challenges, and what the library needs in order to anticipate the future library needs of the city, county, or district. The decision makers then have a choice as to whether to stay with the status quo or to be forward-thinking in their approach to libraries.

Librarians unfortunately cannot expect most decision makers to be forward-thinking unless the librarians themselves are forward-thinking and have already done the appropriate lobbying. A good idea on its own rarely flies. Therefore, librarians must take important prebudget steps with the decision makers so that nothing in the budget is a surprise. With any luck, each of the decision makers will already know the library's needs before the budgetary process begins.

Library Budget Lobbying Techniques

The librarian or library business manager spends several months preparing a budget. The process differs in every library but often begins at the department level with each individual department submitting its needs to the appropriate individual. The next step is compiling the needs and determining the costs to present to the library director or the budget officer. At some point, the library director or budget officer will present the budget to the library board.

After the library board makes its appropriate changes and suggestions, the board or the library director will present it to the appropriate legislative funding body. With planning and good strategy, the librarian should already have involved the decision makers in the budgeting process so that they are generally aware of the library's needs. The most useful elements in acquiring support for the library budget are an understanding of "political pressure points" and the willingness and ability to use them.[17] Political pressure points are lobbying techniques that make a specific decision maker respond as you wish.

Using pressure points effectively can be done in several ways depending on the personalities of the parties involved and, occasionally, on local protocol. Some individuals respond to phone calls from a few prestigious supporters, while others may be more affected by hundreds of library supporters filling the budget hearing room. The library director and the board must know their political funding body and what their pressure points are and must develop an appropriate strategy.[18] For the most part, however, it does not hurt to try a variety of different techniques to see what works.

It is important to get the ear of the decision makers before the actual budget hearings, if possible. The library director and board president may want to invite decision makers out to lunch one at a time. The commissioners, selectmen or selectwomen, or city council members who determine the library's budget are busy, overworked people, but they usually eat lunch. In an informal setting, the librarian can quickly go over the important aspects of the library budget and emphasize areas of greatest importance. Since decision makers often consider librarians individuals with a conflict of interest when it comes to their own budget, it is most effective to have the library board member be the primary spokesperson, with the librarian acting as an informational source.

Another way to provide information to decision makers prior to the budget hearing is to invite the whole group to a very short meeting at the library. They can tour the library to see for themselves the services and the problems that the budget addresses. They should meet with individual staff members who may be able to explain the library's needs more poignantly than the librarian. Often, a picture is worth a thousand detailed budget pages. Seeing forty children attending a story hour in a small area is more powerful than a request for funds to remodel the story hour area. If the librarian calls the meeting an "information reception," an "after business-hours snack and work session," or some other creative name instead of simply an invitation to preview the library's budget, more decision makers may attend. Combining good food and drink with budget information seems to increase a decision maker's willingness to attend.

Finally, as with all public relations and lobbying, the librarian must constantly use imaginative ways to communicate the library's budgetary needs to decision makers. Such communication should be done on a continuing basis throughout the year, not just in the weeks or days before a county commission or city council determines the budget for the year. For example, getting on a town meeting's agenda occasionally throughout the year could be advantageous.

Although lobbying techniques for nonbudgetary issues will be discussed in detail in other chapters, librarians should focus attention on their budgetary needs throughout the year. A very basic, straightforward method is to set up regular meetings with the library board and a committee of the governing structure. For example, in California, a library board committee meets regularly with the community relations committee of the city council.[19] It is also important to have a member of the governing body act as liaison and to have that person attend all library board meetings. Finally, an annual or semiannual meeting even during off-budget years between the governing body and the library can be extremely effective in developing an ongoing relationship. The rapport and understanding between them will already be established when the library needs the support of the governing body.[20]

In addition to solid, practical, no-nonsense interaction between the library and its governing body, there is plenty of room for creativity in the library's approach to informing and thanking individuals who support the library's budget. In West Virginia, the librarians presented pies to every legislator at the capitol or at a "Library Appreciation Day" ceremony, making the most of the theme that librarians "kneaded dough" and part of the funding pie. The campaign was entitled "Library Pie Requires State Dough," and each legislator received a clever recipe book of library facts and figures to go with the pie.[21]

Using holidays as an excuse to contact decision makers throughout the year is certainly appropriate. Christmas cards made or at least signed by all staff members is a nice reminder that the library appreciates its budgetary allocation all year. May Day baskets placed secretly on the doorknobs of council members with information on the library's summer reading program funded by the council and a few fresh flowers will certainly catch the decision maker's attention.

Other government agencies use similar techniques when they place big signs by construction projects stating, "This Is Your One Percent Sales Tax at Work." Librarians should utilize similar big signs on remodeling or building projects, and new collections or services. The sign could read, "This New Collection Is Provided by Your County Commissioners." Such a sign would serve not only to thank the funding body for its additional support but also to remind the public how a library is funded. You can then elicit public support to push the political pressure points of the legislative body in the future.

Decision makers should also receive special invitations to events the library sponsors during the year, both for the public and for library staff members. Invite them to your Christmas party, your volunteer recognition dinner, your board tea, and introduce them at all of these functions as VIPs, giving them the kudos they deserve for supporting the library's budget. Send them a library card on their birthday or give them a birthday certificate good for two free copies on the library's copier, or a free video for the night, or a free coupon for a meeting room. The list goes on and on and only stops when a creative library staff's imagination is exhausted.

In addition, if the library or the friends publish a newsletter, the decision makers should receive a copy. Librarians should also send copies of board minutes to decision makers. Don't be afraid of revealing too much and don't try to conceal the library's inner workings. Don't worry that the library is sending decision makers too much. Decision makers receive a lot of information from many groups and are good at skimming and tossing information quickly. However, they will remember that the library included them, and they will remember that the library is active and involved in the community, even if they don't remember details.

Planning a Lobbying Effort

Laying the Foundation

The first step in laying a foundation to begin lobbying is to identify the decision makers who directly affect your library's needs, budgetary or otherwise. A public librarian must know the names, addresses, and backgrounds of local decision makers, such as the city council, mayor, city manager, or county commissioners.

A librarian should keep a file (easiest on a computer) on all of these decision makers, recording their likes and dislikes, interests, and avocations. The file should contain dates of all important interactions the librarian, board, or staff members have had with that decision maker. Immediately after such an interaction, the library representatives should jot down pertinent personal facts as well as information about library issues that were discussed and enter it into the decision maker's file. The librarian should keep copies of all correspondence between the decision maker and the library. The librarian should review this file, the letters, and the personal notes before meeting with the decision maker again in order to remember what transpired in previous interactions. The information will give the librarian a basis of conversation on topics about the decision maker's family or interests. The librarian can use the list of topical interests to inform the decision maker about a new publication or program at the library that might be of interest to that person.

Information on key library votes should also be maintained in the file, so that if a decision maker changes his or her position on a library issue, the librarian will know it immediately and can approach the decision maker for information about the vote.

Key Players

All the key players in an organized, thoughtful lobbying effort have a variety of responsibilities in common. As this book will mention repeatedly, a primary duty of all the players—from the library director to the friends—is to maintain a close and meaningful relationship with the local government administration, its elected officials, and the electorate that provides the taxes to support the library.[22] These kinds of relationships do not develop overnight, and they do not happen without planning. Many individuals play a role in a good lobbying effort, and each should be aware of his or her unique responsibilities.

HEAD LIBRARIAN/LIBRARY DIRECTOR

The head librarian sets the stage for an effective lobbying effort and serves as an example to others who also represent the library in one capacity or another. A primary responsibility of the director is to orchestrate the lobbying effort. The director must have the appropriate overview of the library's needs, who or what group can fulfill those needs, and what role individuals connected with the library can play. With that goal in mind, the director plans and coordinates the library's lobbying program.

The director can delegate much of the plan to others. However, it is so important to have one voice (not one person, but all individuals saying the same thing) that someone must be responsible for the message. The director knows most intimately the library's budget and the potential nonbudget issues facing it. It is therefore imperative that the director annually assess the political needs of the library and make a written plan of attack.

The plan should begin as an outline of the library's needs in the first column, who or what body can provide those needs in the second column, how the library plans to obtain each need in the third column, and the persons needed to implement the plan in the fourth column. A date for achieving each objective should be set, and the director should begin working with the appropriate individuals to achieve the library's goals. More strategy in this area will be discussed below.

LIBRARY BOARD OF TRUSTEES

Although the head librarian is certainly an important person in orchestrating the library's lobbying effort, the most powerful group of lobbyists associated with the library is the board of trustees. The board is extremely credible to the elected officials, unlike paid staff and the library director who are considered to have a vested interest as employees. The trustees' willingness to serve without compensation demonstrates their strong belief in the value of a library. No one is in a better position than the board of trustees to motivate and mobilize other community leaders and groups to lobby actively for the library.[23]

Library board members are public officials in their own right and represent the community at large. They were appointed or elected with a mandate to work in the interest of the library and to represent the public served by the library. Although they see the library from the public's point of view, they also have a working knowledge of the library's operations.[24] They are therefore ideal lobbyists who have nothing personal to gain from their advocacy— the kind of lobbyist to which decision makers pay a lot of attention.

Library trustees have a tremendous responsibility in the library's ongoing lobbying effort. They must make sure that the local governing officials understand the library's needs, problems, and role in the community. Many people still think of libraries as storehouses for books. With increasing literacy programs, advanced technology, and well-trained librarians and staff, libraries can more successfully compete for dollars with so-called essential services. Trustees must be able to communicate effectively to the funding body what the library offers today to its citizens.

However, no library board can claim effective working relationships with its funding body unless the trustees regularly sit down and talk amicably and not defensively with the decision makers about the library's budgets and programs.[25] Such talks can be incorporated into library board meetings if a representative from the local funding body attends them. A representative from the library board should attend meetings of the funding body and occasionally ask for time on its agenda. If such regular interaction does not exist, trustees can set up a quarterly or biannual meeting with the governing body to discuss library issues. Once such meetings are established, the funding body begins to incorporate them into its own schedule and comes with questions it develops itself.

Several state library trustee manuals provide excellent guidelines to help trustees who lobby.[26] The California manual provides some "basic guidelines from experienced trustees" about working with public officials. A few of these are listed below.

1. Trustees should not be intimidated or in awe of public officials because they, too, are public officials and therefore on an equal footing.
2. Trustees must all express the same basic message.
3. Trustees should get acquainted with each "power-hierarchy" official to determine that person's stance and voting record on library issues, especially the budget.
4. Trustees should be "conversantly familiar" with local, state, and federal laws affecting the library, and should attend the meetings of the governing body frequently.
5. Instead of talking to decision makers about the *library's* needs, phrase the concerns in terms of "*your constituents'* needs" or the *people's* needs.
6. Maintain regular and periodic communications instead of waiting until budget time to approach decision makers.[27]

The library trustee who meets with members of the funding body must be absolutely sold on the value of libraries in general and on his or her library in particular. The library trustee must also be well-informed about the library's budgetary needs and not have to rely on the library director or budget officer to present details to the funding body. Although a trustee must take a lot of time to learn what is necessary to represent the library well, when the final dollar figures come in, the reward is well worth the effort.

LIBRARY STAFF

The library staff is on the front lines and is a "large, highly skilled potential political advocate."[28] Staff members deal with the public and public officials on a continual one-to-one basis. The political importance of their dealings with the public is that if the library builds a strong constituency base, good relations with the public will provide the library with a tremendously powerful lobbying force.[29]

On the other hand, the staff needs to be low-key in any lobbying effort. As people paid with tax dollars, they are considered individuals with a vested interest. If an elected official believes that library staff members are lobbying or advocating for the library when they should be "doing their job," that perception may hurt the library's efforts.

The main role of a staff member, other than the director, is to provide the best service possible at all times, although the staff is involved to some extent in the overall political scheme. At the very least, all staff members who greet the public should know their elected officials, staff, and other key individuals by name and by face. When these individuals actually use the library, they should get VIP treatment. Staff members should address them by name before looking at their cards and make special efforts to determine if they are finding what they need. Along these lines and by way of example, the motel where most legislators stay in Wyoming when the legislature is in session gives its employees written tests on identifying legislators. They are required to learn the faces along with the names of every legislator so that the legislators feel at home and important when they interact with staff in the lobby, in the restaurant, at the registration desk, etc. It is good policy.

FRIENDS OF THE LIBRARY

Friends of the library provide a "bulk" that the library staff and board alone cannot. They can help promote budget proposals, work on bond issue campaigns, join the effort to change state statutes affecting public libraries, and so on. The list is endless. When letters to decision makers are required, the friends are the perfect individuals to do the writing.

When personal phone calls are necessary, friends again should be put to use. Telephone communications with elected officials can be tricky, however, so the friends who call must be informed adequately or the phone call may be damaging instead of effective.

Friends can also be helpful when a large showing at a committee hearing or a budget presentation is necessary. In this capacity, they need only sit there with their library t-shirts, pins, or other identifying mark. They make a statement by their presence. More recommendations on phone calls, letters, and attending committees are found in other Chapter 4 of this book.

As with all other aspects of lobbying, the librarian-lobbyist must establish and solidify the relationship with these community supporters before the end of the fiscal year when the budget hearing nears or when they are needed in other campaign areas. In other words, you need to lobby the friends to lobby the decision makers.

THE PRESS

An often overlooked key player in lobbying is the press. The press is not the library's enemy, and it can be the library's best friend. The press can help lobby elected officials in two ways. First, it can educate them about the problems the library is having. A conscientious decision maker reads his or her local and state newspapers with a keen eye for public opinion. Especially important are the letters to the editor and any front page story depicting a problem, especially when it involves something in the decision maker's political domain. Decision makers listen to the radio news and watch television news for stories about issues of import to their constituencies. If they do not, when they receive calls and letters, they may not know what is happening. In fact, when a legislature is in session, sometimes the only information the house or assembly receives about what happened in the senate (and vice versa) is from the press. The most dramatic example of the key role the press can play in educating both decision makers and the public was seen in the Gulf War, during which Iraqi government officials, United States government officials, and everyone else in the world who had access to a television watched Cable News Network.

The second way the press can affect public official decision making is by controlling how a decision maker is depicted to the public. Public officials are extremely sensitive to what the press says about them and how they are portrayed in the public eye. Most elected officials do not like negative press (although politicians are told to get their names in front of the public as often as possible—even if only for getting a speeding ticket—since the public forgets why it knows a name). Nevertheless, if decision makers can avoid looking bad in the press, they will try to do so. On the other hand, if a library lobbyist can convince a decision maker that going out on a limb for the library will provide the person with excellent press, that person may be willing to do so. Very few individuals inherently dislike libraries, and therefore many politicians consider them safe bets. It nevertheless may take a lot of convincing by the librarian before elected officials will embrace a library issue publicly as their own.

The press can make the library a public and positive issue, it can ignore the library, or it can uncover and play upon conflicts involving the library. In any lobbying effort, good relations with the press must be established immediately if they are not already in place. The library should not wait until there is a problem to develop good press relations.[30] Knowing individual reporters by name and keeping them informed on everything important are good ways to guarantee coverage and accurate reporting.[31] Librarians should not lobby the press per se, but involving the press is an integral and critical part of a good library lobbying campaign.

KEY ADMINISTRATORS AND OTHER
LOCAL OFFICIALS

Librarians should identify key administrative staff members of the governing body and others in key positions of power. These people can be developed into library friends and allies. They can provide important information and advice to the library board and speak in support of the library as they work with the governing officials and the city or county departments.[32]

Depending on the governance structure of the library, these people can include the city manager, the mayor, the county chief administrative officer, the budget officer, the planning department, the purchasing officer, the city or county clerk, the legal officer, the secretaries of all of the above, and others.[33] In some situations, these individuals serve in a decision-making capacity, in which case they are discussed in the next section on decision makers. However, if the city manager, for example, acts *ex officio* as an informational, nonvoting member of a city council that makes the budgetary decisions, it is good to get that person's confidence early on. Often, informal talk between these individuals and the elected officials may persuade the undecided or fence-riding decision maker to decide on behalf of the library.

Librarians should try to determine on which individual or individuals the decision makers rely for a sense of the community. Remember, elected officials have only a limited amount of time and cannot be expected to know everything about everything. They must lean heavily on someone if they have not had the opportunity to do the homework necessary to make an informed decision. Their advisors, both informal and formal, are important allies for the library lobbyist to groom.

THE DECISION MAKERS THEMSELVES

Vital to any decision that affects libraries are the people who make the decisions. They have a tremendous responsibility to attempt to meet the needs of the public when they can determine what the needs are, and to be responsive to the will of the public. Many librarians take for granted that decision makers somehow know how they will vote on an issue even if they have little or no information about it. This is a correct assessment in many cases. Decision makers must make hundreds of individual decisions and votes, and they cannot be experts in everything.

However, they are usually grateful when they receive information that helps them make a better-informed decision. They also are grateful when they receive communications from the public they represent about an issue they have to decide. If they do not receive constituent input, they assume that the issue is not controversial or that no one cares. If they hear from a handful of individuals, they will pay close attention to their comments and often follow the recommendation. If they hear from many individuals on both sides of an issue with which they are not familiar, they are then faced with needing additional information and discussing the issue with individuals they trust. A small group of vocal librarians can make a big difference in the way a decision maker votes.

Every decision maker and elected official makes "wrong" votes that they regret later. They make bad votes usually as a result of lack of information or lack of timely input by the people a decision affects. Library advocates should therefore feel good about providing decision makers with information so that the decision makers will not ultimately regret and be embarrassed about a particular vote.

Library trustees can conceivably fall under the definition of "decision makers" as used in the context of this book. Library trustees are decision makers if they are trustees of a library district or elected trustees of a public library board. As such, they are accountable to constituents, especially when they are elected. Friends of the library will officially lobby them, and the library director must take a slightly different tack when dealing with them as decision makers.

Another important consideration about decision makers who are also key players is that decision makers lobby one another. Perhaps the most powerful lobbyists are fellow elected officials. In most states, it is unlawful to trade votes. However, legislators feel a tremendous camaraderie among themselves because they are all experiencing the same situation, i.e., they have a common bond. As military veterans knowingly speak with one another, as women who have gone through childbirth have empathy for one another, so do battle-scarred, weary legislators and elected officials speak persuasively with one another because of the commonality of their experience.

If a librarian can develop a good relationship with a decision maker and win a library ally and advocate, the results can be excellent. For example, I felt like a librarian disguised as a legislator for many years because I was in the unique position of having the ear of all the other elected officials on matters relating to libraries. I have discussed the importance of libraries and the need to fund them at every opportunity with any colleague who would listen. As a direct result, legislators became more aware of libraries and more positive about them.

The First Efforts

As with all "firsts," expect that everything that can go wrong will go wrong. Experience in lobbying helps, but it never makes a political situation perfect. The players keep changing, so something that worked predictably well with one person may not work at all on that person's replacement.

All library directors have lobbied decision makers in one capacity or another, even if the lobbying was unintentional or not thought of as lobbying. If a library director has never consciously done any lobbying, however, the first step is to figure out what your library needs and wants and who can help meet those needs. The library should have both an annual lobbying plan with goals and a long-term lobbying plan. The library may have no particular needs that can be solved by a legislative body other than annual budgetary needs. Intense lobbying campaigns should be saved for commensurate needs, such as large increases in budget, changes in state legislation affecting libraries, or special one-time needs such as a new building. Overkill is counterproductive.

The director should communicate his or her recommendations for a library lobbying plan to the library's governing board so that the trustees can become conversant with the library's political goals and add, delete, or alter the plan as they see fit.

Once the librarian and board determine the library's needs and goals, the next step is to begin preparing informational files on the decision makers who affect the library. This kind of information is available through the League of Women Voters, through publications by other groups or by the government body itself, through the newspapers, and through old-fashioned sleuthing and word of mouth. Often the best information will come from "friends of friends" or from unexpected sources.

After becoming acquainted with these individuals on paper, the library director and trustees should then personally acquaint themselves with each elected official. The best way to accomplish this is to simply call the official's office to schedule a meeting with the decision maker. Details about initial contact are found in Chapter 4.

At the first meeting, the library director or trustee should outline the library's concerns and needs and express the library's appreciation of the decision maker's willingness to meet with the library. If the library has no current pressing agenda, it is perfectly legitimate (and in fact, probably more effective in the long run) to simply say that you wanted to meet the decision maker in order to open lines of communication. Decision makers appreciate meeting a constituent without an agenda at times. After the meeting, the trustee and librarian should send a short thank-you note expressing appreciation for the meeting and letting the decision maker know they will be in touch again soon.

This kind of one-on-one contact is time-consuming but worthwhile. A face now accompanies the name of the politician. The politician now also has a name and face to call upon when questions concerning the library arise. This is an important step forward and a basic one in any lobbying effort.

The next step involves working with the library staff. Once the library board affirms the library's political goals, the library director should communicate these goals to the library staff. The staff should be trained in how to deal with decision makers. When the staff knows what is expected of them, then they can effectively begin their campaign with the public and with elected officials who actually use the library.

Friends must then be filled in, especially if immediate action is required. The library lobbyist should let the friends of the library know the library's plan. The friends should be given notice that they may be needed to help in certain ways. Some individuals feel uncomfortable making telephone calls, while others don't like to write letters. The librarian should determine who likes to do what and develop a list of names under each category of needs so that the people are ready to do what they like at the drop of a hat.

Finally, if appropriate, the news media should be alerted about what the library intends to do. They should be the last to be called, although if a newspaper has a "stringer" assigned to the library board, the press would have picked up the story much earlier. But before any plan is published in the paper, the library board should have approved it, the library staff should be fully informed, and if at all possible, the elected officials should know about it. Prior knowledge of the plan will make the decision makers feel as if they are a part of it.

Occasionally an elected official will say something that is critical of the library. Under no circumstances should a librarian or library supporter criticize the decision maker in the press or privately, unless a library representative first contacts the elected official to determine what happened. Often, bad feelings can be avoided and a friend made if the elected official is asked in private to explain why he or she voted in a certain way or said something about the library that was negative. Also, if the press misquoted the elected official or misunderstood his or her action, attacking the decision maker will only aggravate the situation. I was misquoted by the press regarding a school administration. Even after I explained my comments to the administration in person, the attorney for the school wrote me a subtly intimidating letter. In my opinion, this action was out of line, in poor taste, and showed a lack of political acumen on the part of the attorney.

In summary, the first steps in establishing a lobbying effort involve "lining up your ducks." Know what the library wants and needs, get those needs approved by the appropriate individuals, alert all parties to the plan, alert the media to the plan, and then begin implementation.

The Follow-Up

Even as you implement your plan, the library director and trustees should be aware of appropriate closures or finishing touches. Every interaction of any kind with a legislator should be followed by a short note from the librarian to the legislator. If you took the elected official out to lunch, send a note thanking the official for taking the time to eat with you. It's a good idea in this case to thank the decision maker for your treat.

If you are denied funding or the ordinance you wanted failed, ask the decision maker what happened. The answers may surprise as well as disappoint you. When beginning a dialogue regarding a failed effort, the librarian should not be defensive or accusatory. The best learning experience can sometimes come from a postmortem conversation with decision makers. Remember also that it often takes a good idea time to catch on. Ordinances and legislation can be introduced over and over again. There is always another session or another meeting. If you feel defeated after a loss, you are defeated. By understanding the process of which defeat is a part, the librarian will realize that a defeat simply means a little more work must be done next time.

Unfortunately, defeat in certain areas cannot be made up by future requests. Certainly budget losses are the worst, and insufficient funding will mean lost opportunity. Even so, you need the decision makers' votes again and again on other matters, so do not isolate those persons because you lose once. Also, when decision makers know that you are still concerned after you lose a vote, they will remember that. However, if the officials do not see you again until right before your next budget request, the chances for a repeat performance of failure are higher. Continue your lobbying efforts throughout the year so that decision makers will know you are still concerned about funding.

If you are successful in your effort, follow your success with publicity, as previously mentioned. The librarian should draft a press release for the local paper (or call a press conference if that is the preferred method in your area) and call the local radio stations. Newspapers will not pick up everything, but if the librarian has developed a good working relationship with the press, a newspaper will probably publish a short article and recognize the efforts of the local decision maker.

The Long-term Plan

Although some library issues appear unexpectedly, the librarian should be able to anticipate the major issues facing the library at the local level and prepare for them in advance. Prepare a five-year tentative lobbying plan and revise it each year as necessary. The plan can be flexible, but it must exist.

Notes

1. Cecil Beach, "Local Funding of Public Libraries," *Library Journal* 110 (15 June 1985): 28; Virgil L. P. Blake, "Library and Municipal Officials: The Great Divide," *The Bottom Line* 3, no. 2 (1989): 28, reprinted in *The Leadership Role of Library Trustees: 4th Annual Trustee Institute* (Harrisburg: State Library of Pennsylvania, Pennsylvania Library Association Trustee Division, May 11 and 12, 1990); Betty Bay, ed., *Trustee Tool Kit for Library Leadership* (Sacramento: California State Library, 1987).

2. Marilyn Gell Mason, "Politics and the Public Library: A Management Guide," *Library Journal* 114 (15 March 1989): 27.

3. Beach, "Local Funding of Public Libraries," 28.

4. Mason, "Politics and the Public Library: A Management Guide," 28.

5. Betty Bay, ed., *Trustee Tool Kit for Library Leadership*, 25–26.

6. Ibid.

7. Suzan Rickert, *Campaigning for Libraries*, ed. Judy Zelenski (Wheat Ridge: The Central Colorado Library System, 1988).

8. Ibid., 28.

9. Ibid., 28–29.

10. Ibid., 29–30.

11. Ibid., 30.

12. Ibid., 28.

13. Beach, "Local Funding of Public Libraries," 27.

14. Ibid.

15. Mason, "Politics and the Public Library: A Management Guide," 31.

16. Ibid., 29.

17. Ibid.

18. Ibid.

19. Betty Bay, ed., *Trustee Tool Kit for Library Leadership*, 177.

20. Ibid.

21. Frederick J. Glazer, "Legislative Tips," in *Prepare! The Library Public Relations Recipe Book*, ed. Irene E. Moran (Chicago: Public Relations Section, Library Administrative and Management Association, American Library Association, 1978), 47.

22. Beach, "Local Funding of Public Libraries," 28.

23. Betty Bay, ed., *Trustee Tool Kit for Library Leadership*, 193–94.

24. Ibid., 174.

25. Ibid., 172.

26. Although I quote frequently from these manuals, interested trustees

may want to borrow copies of other states' trustee manuals for additional tips and ideas.

27. Betty Bay, ed., *Trustee Tool Kit for Library Leadership*, 177–80.
28. Ibid.
29. Neel Parikh, "Organizing for Political Change," *Library Journal* 105, no. 12 (15 June 1980): 1365.
30. Mason, "Politics and the Public Library: A Management Guide," 30.
31. Parikh, "Organizing for Political Change," 1364–65.
32. Betty Bay, ed., *Trustee Tool Kit for Library Leadership*, 180–81.
33. Ibid., 181.

8

Lobbying for Schools

Typical Funding Sources

Education is funded through a partnership of local, state, and federal governments. In 1970, on a national average, the local share was 52.5 percent, the state share was 39.1 percent and the federal share was 8.4 percent. During the last twenty years, the funding sources have remained basically the same, but the state has become the greatest source of funds. In 1990, the local share was 44.1 percent, the state share was 49.6 percent, and the federal share dropped to 6.3 percent.[1] Sources of funding include local sales, property, and other taxes, and direct state aid. Supplemental sources are sometimes available from the state library, from the state department of education, from federal government agencies, or from nongovernmental sources, such as private foundations or businesses. A thorough discussion of federal sources is found in Chapter 1.

The amount of money an individual school district receives affects the amount of money that a school media center receives. The library receives a percentage of the total amount of the school's budget. This amount varies from school to school as well as from state to state.

Librarians and teachers also look to outside sources to supplement their budgets. Many enterprising teachers and librarians apply for grants from businesses and foundations for "extras" the students might not otherwise have available to them, such as computers, giveaway books, VCRs, and so on.

Even though funding for school media centers comes from all levels of government, the actual dollar amount to be spent by a school district on libraries is often determined at the local level, by the principal, the superintendent of the district, and the school board. If the librarian is a district media coordinator, then he or she most likely will approach a superintendent or school board first for funding. A building-level librarian usually works with the principal in determining a budget.

Different statutory schemes determine how much a school district receives and who makes decisions on how to allocate its total dollar amount. In some states, educational reform allows a council consisting of parents, teachers, and administrators to make decisions. Some states are experimenting with "site-based budgeting" by which funding decisions are made at the building level rather than at the state level. If implemented, this approach could give the building-level librarian more influence over how much the school media centers would receive. Other state laws provide financial rewards and sanctions based on school performance.[2] The policy of "choice," by which parents choose which school they want their children to attend, also affects the funding level of schools within a district. Many states adhere to a strong policy of local control over funding priorities once the money is distributed. The school librarian should know all potential funding sources and exactly who makes the decisions on funding.

Lobbying for school and academic libraries is more complicated than for public libraries because decision makers allocate funds first for the cost of "education."[3] Instructional media centers are still usually included as part of the "auxiliary" services in many school budgets. An appallingly small percentage of the overall budget is spent on media center acquisitions, personnel, or overhead. Often an instructional media center seems to be an afterthought and a low priority for budgetary allotment. As an example of the misperceptions sometimes associated with media centers, the popular movie *The Breakfast Club* depicts the school media center as a place to punish children instead of the focus of the educational institution as it ought to be.

In addition, many states are battling over equitable funding for education to prevent schools in one part of a state from receiving more funding to educate their students simply because of their geographical location. For example, in Wyoming in 1983, the school funding scheme was declared unconstitutional by the Wyoming supreme court.[4] As a result, the state had to implement a new school funding scheme, which has been fine-tuned and adjusted annually since then. Another suit was filed early in 1992 by four Wyoming school districts claiming that the state had impoverished the richer districts in its attempt to achieve financial equity. Many other states have also implemented new school funding schemes, including Kentucky, Nebraska, New Jersey, Montana, and Texas, among others.[5] In 1989, the Kentucky supreme court ordered the general assembly to devise an entirely new educational structure. The ruling applied to state and local systems of financing education, the structure of school districts and school boards, school construction and maintenance, and teacher certification.[6] The decision was based on a suit filed by sixty-six of the poorest school districts in the state who claimed that their students did not receive substantially equal educational opportunities compared with other schools in the state.[7] The result was a 924-page educational reform bill that included a tax increase for Kentucky citizens and a substantial increase in state aid to the poorer school districts.[8] The Texas legislature met in four special sessions before it passed a new school funding plan in June 1990. In April 1990, the Nebraska legislature increased state aid to public schools from 25 to 45 percent.[9]

In states where a new funding schedule is being established because of a court or other mandate, librarians must lobby hard in the early stages so that media centers are not forgotten in the melee. In fact, because instructional media centers are almost uniformly underfunded within a school district, the school library lobbyist must argue strongly that this is where new money should be allocated. School reform provides a unique opportunity for the school library. It potentially gives school librarians at both the building level and the district level the chance to have a voice in restructuring the funding priorities within a school district. Although much of school-funding reform involves distribution of state monies to a school district as opposed to reallocation of money within a district after it is received, statewide educational reform provides an excellent opportunity to fight for new district-funding priorities. The school-library lobbyist must be an assertive, active participant in this process. When committees are formed, the school-library lobbyist must always insist that a representative from the library, not just a teacher, be appointed to it. Be sure to volunteer if representatives from local school districts are needed to testify to state legislative committees. If town meetings or public hearings are planned, get on the agenda to speak about libraries. Take advantage of the required rethinking of allocation of funds to increase funding for the media center.

As the school-library lobbyist becomes involved in these events, he or she must have the support of the principal at the building level or the superintendent or school board at the district media level. Although it is theoretically true that the more money a school district receives, the greater the likelihood that a school media center within that district will receive additional funding, the library lobbyist still must make the case, justify the need, negotiate any increase with the principal or superintendent, and lobby accordingly.

In states that are not dealing with educational reforms, lobbying remains tough. Because instructional media centers are part of a larger educational institution and not the primary focus of budgetary priorities, the building-level librarian associated with library media centers has to work doubly hard to plan and execute a lobbying effort. If school districts are not being scrutinized as a result of a court order, and if no strong movement exists to examine funding priorities, the school-library lobbyist must try to create a little furor and excitement about the library media center without these advantages.

Profile of a Typical Decision Maker

Lobbying for a school library is different from lobbying for a public library because of the complex decision-making hierarchy in the schools. The power hierarchy in the educational setting tremendously affects the school librarian's lobbying strategy. The building-level librarian is located at the bottom of the hierarchy, followed by the building principal, a business manager or assistant superintendent, the district superintendent, and then the final decision makers—the school board or the state legislature. The titles and hierarchy will vary from state to state. A district media coordinator may be under the direct supervision of a superintendent and have more direct interaction with a school board than a building-level librarian. The size of a city may also make a difference. A building-level librarian in a small town will often lobby school board members or legislators informally, and all parties involved consider such interaction appropriate. In a larger city, the building-level librarian may not know who the decision makers are and, in any case, lobbying on the librarian's part would be considered unacceptable. Even the district coordinator may not be empowered to lobby the legislature. School-library lobbyists must always determine what is appropriate within their own school districts before they act.

Because so many individuals are involved in the hierarchy, the librarian must determine who makes the real decisions. Does the school board simply rubber-stamp the budget or does it go over every item and make independent judgments on funding? Does the superintendent accept all of the recommendations of the business manager? Does the business manager or assistant superintendent in charge of finance accept all of the principal's recommendations? Does the principal ask the librarian for a detailed budget or does the media center always get what it got last year? Where must the librarian-lobbyist assert pressure to make a difference?

Decisions and priorities are often made at each level, and it may be difficult to determine the most powerful person or persons within the hierarchy. None of the individuals, including the person who finally makes recommendations to the elected decision makers, is elected. Instead, these people are employees of the school district. They include the principal or assistant principal in charge of finance, the superintendent or assistant superintendent, the business or budget manager, or others, depending on the structure of your school district. At least one of them, usually the principal, is the direct supervisor of the building-level school librarian. This structure makes lobbying doubly difficult for a school librarian.

Nonelected decision makers in an educational situation include individuals whose job descriptions typically require them to make budgetary decisions affecting libraries or media centers within a school district. They must know and understand budgets thoroughly. How do they then differ from the elected decision makers? The nonelected decision makers do not need to keep a constituency happy in order to keep their jobs. Simplistically, they just need to keep their immediate supervisors happy. School librarians may have a harder time lobbying the nonelected decision makers than the elected decision makers because no constituency base exists to help lobby and apply pressure. Part of keeping an immediate supervisor happy may mean being frugal with a budget and cutting corners where possible. The nonelected decision maker also may have to worry about unhappy teachers, support personnel, and administrators who did not receive their full budget request. The library media center is competing with money for classes, sports programs, and all the other requirements within a school district, and the nonelected decision maker may make the first cuts.

Internal administrative battles often must be fought before a request reaches the elected decision makers. The principal may be extremely supportive of the librarian's program, but the superintendent may have different priorities, or vice versa. The librarian may be in a political situation that limits his or her lobbying efforts to only the building principal. Lobbying the superintendent directly may be perceived by the principal as going around the principal's authority in order to influence budgetary priorities. If so, the librarian must lobby that decision maker well enough so that the principal will lobby the next appropriate level on behalf of the library. A chain reaction of lobbying never hurts: a school-library lobbyist convinces the principal, who convinces the budget manager, who convinces the superintendent, who convinces the school board, which convinces the state legislature. Luckily, the district coordinator will have fewer levels to convince, but the same philosophy applies.

A typical elected decision maker in an educational setting is a part-time school board member whose primary occupation is something other than the elected position he or she holds. He or she is directly responsible to an electorate and can be voted out of office if the public decides it does not like the board member's decisions. The school board will most often make the final overall budgetary decisions, although a domineering administrator may influence the board's decision greatly. The board might also be responsible for determining the actual dollar amount allocated for media centers within a district. School boards are structured differently from district to district. They usually are not directly involved in the hiring or firing of the school media specialist, although when budget crises exist, they may eliminate a library position and, in essence, relieve the librarian of his or her job. Know which members within the school board are the most pwerful and influential and if any are connected with libraries in any way. Under most state laws, school boards must meet and make their decisions publicly. They therefore have an added element of credibility that some school administrators lack.

Part of the school-library lobbyist's homework is to determine what role the school board plays. The school-library lobbyist must be aware of any rules the school district has governing interactions by school employees with the school board. A school district in a rural area where everyone knows everyone else may be more relaxed about interactions than one in a larger urban area. A school librarian must involve the parents in dealing with the school board if school policy limits his or her interaction with the school board.

Occasionally an issue requires a decision at the state or federal level. The library media specialist must first determine under what authority (school policy, school board resolution, state law, state department of education rule, federal law, etc.) a decision maker is acting. When it appears that the school board is implementing an onerous state or federal requirement, the school-library lobbyist has to lobby more than the decision makers at the local level in order to change the law. The school-library lobbyist must then deal with state legislators or federal senators or representatives. Other sections of this book deal with how to interact with those individuals.

Typical Budgetary Profile and Problems

Many of the tips on lobbying for public library budgets may be useful for the school-library media specialist when preparing a budget request. The school librarian should prepare a detailed breakdown of all of the library's needs based on current researched costs and justification of those needs. The individuals scrutinizing the school librarian's proposed budget are very familiar with the budget needs of the school or system, so it is important that the detailed document be as thorough and accurate as possible. This situation is in contrast to decision makers in a public library setting who may not have as thorough an understanding of the library's budgetary needs. Although the school librarian should also prepare an easy-to-read one-page summary of the proposed budget, the summary may not be used until the school board receives it as part of a packet of budget information.

Planning a Lobbying Effort

Laying the Foundation

As mentioned above, the school-library lobbyist must determine where the power lies at every level of decision making. Once the school-library lobbyist has identified the power decision makers, the next thing to do is to get to know them on a personal basis. As suggested earlier in the book in the context of public libraries, the school librarian should compile information about those individuals—from their educational backgrounds to their likes and dislikes. Although it may not be possible to befriend them or officially lobby them, it is appropriate to include them in library activities. Invite them to do a book talk or speak on one of their hobbies during a week celebrating that hobby or during National Library Week. Invite them to visit a class where you are instructing students on how to use the library media center. Computer technology may be especially impressive. Send them your newsletter if you have one and send them announcements of all activities in the library media center that you think might be of interest. The more knowledge they have about your program, the better. Eat lunch with them or invite them to the library to discuss library issues with you before budget time, so that when it is time to do the budgets, the decision makers are familiar with the library's problems.

School librarians sometimes hesitate to lobby for fear of losing their jobs. Yet lobbying is an integral part of their responsibilities. It is important that a school library have everything it needs to be as effective as possible. If a school media center is constantly short of personnel and money for acquisitions, or if the facilities are woefully inadequate, it is the library media specialist's responsibility to communicate these needs to the appropriate individuals.

School librarians cannot be faulted for communicating their needs in a friendly, informative, continuous manner. In fact, many administrators will consider a person with this kind of initiative an effective employee. I have, however, talked to many school librarians over the years who have insisted that their administrators would be threatened by lobbying activities on their part and that the best way to survive is to keep quiet. Certainly insecure administrators exist, and the librarian runs the risk of threatening one. Recently, when two teachers criticized central administration publicly, they were observed in their classrooms for two hours in an intimidation attempt the following day. Such outlandish behavior on the part of school administrators is, fortunately, infrequent. In this case, in my opinion, the behavior of the administration indicates that it deserved the criticism!

Part of a school librarian's lobbying homework is to determine the temperament of the administrators with whom they work. They should also discover whether or not any previous school librarians had problems stemming from their activities of promoting the school library. The school librarian should not limit his or her own activities simply because no one has ever lobbied before. However, the librarian should be sensitive to whether an administrator finds the lobbying activities troublesome. The librarian-lobbyist may decide to reevaluate his or her plan and curtail or limit lobbying activities if they aggravate the administrator. Perhaps being more subtle is all that is required. Remember that librarians have first amendment rights protecting their freedom of speech. On the other hand, if it looks as if a well-planned lobbying effort is working or at least no one is complaining, keep it up and build on it. Establishing a strong relationship with and informing administrators about the school media center will pay off tremendously in the long run.

A school librarian will want to establish a support group of interested parents as soon as possible. Parents are the best group to lobby decision makers because of the general perception that librarians or teachers have a vested interest in receiving additional funding, even if it is for nonsalary needs. A support group is a good idea in any case, but it is essential if the school librarian feels uncomfortable developing relationships with decision makers or believes it is inappropriate to do so. A parental support group must be formed far enough in advance of a problem so that articulate, knowledgeable individuals can represent the school library on the spur of the moment. If an emergency arises and a support group is not already in existence, the librarian may have to form and educate a group quickly.

This group can be an effective lobbying force, although there are always dangers associated with any kind of group like this. First, depending on the school district, the school librarian may or may not be able to organize and participate actively in such a group. Without such guidance, the support group could become the antithesis of what the library needs, i.e., a parental group that wants to limit reading materials for students. On the other hand, it is important that the group be somewhat independent of the wishes of the librarian so that it will remain credible to decision makers. Once established, a strong parental support group could be invaluable to the school librarian in many areas. Again, the group should be formed before problems arise, so that when the library needs help the support group is ready to take action.

Another parental group that may already be established and can be very helpful to elementary school media centers is the Parent Teacher Association (PTA) or Parent Teacher Organization (PTO). The librarian needs to educate the members of the PTA or PTO about the needs of the school media center annually so that this group might endorse specific school media programs as well as programs for the school as a whole.

Key Players Who Lobby

THE SCHOOL LIBRARIANS

The term *school librarian* is out of vogue. In this book it is used to mean the top administrative librarian at the building level or the top administrative librarian in a school district. Certainly other important library positions play a support role similar to that of public library staff members (excluding the director). However, because of the complex power structure within a school setting, they do not have as much visibility as their public library counterparts.

Historically, school librarians are not aggressive about fighting for funding because of the fear of losing their jobs. Whether such an outcome is perceived or real, a school librarian may resist putting pressure on a nonelected decision maker if that person also has a say in the librarian's continued employment.

Nevertheless, after some background work, the school librarian may find that the first step is to focus lobbying efforts primarily on his or her immediate supervisor. For the building-level librarian, this is the principal. For the district media coordinator, this is often the superintendent. The librarian should regularly inform that person about the school media center following other suggestions in this book and involve that person when possible in the day-to-day activities in the school library. Your primary goal is to gain the confidence of that person so that you can work your way up the hierarchy to whoever makes the actual monetary decisions about the school media center. The power individual or individuals could be any of those previously mentioned. Once you know whom you need to influence and how the power structure within your district works, then you develop a strategy to allow you to lobby without fear.

THE PARENTS

The parents can play a major role in lobbying the appropriate people, from the principal to the school board. They have the most influence over an elected school board because elected officials must be responsible to their electorate. Principals and superintendents certainly hope to maintain the goodwill of parents, but school administrators do not usually report directly to the parents. Instead, they must keep the school board happy. Parents, therefore, are most effective in dealing with the school board, although they should still voice their opinions to the principal and superintendent. On the other hand, if it appears that the parents have a gripe with certain administrators and they want the school board to straighten it out, the school board will often back its administrators' decisions. The school-library lobbyist must work closely and thoughtfully with parents to develop a strategy to increase library media center funding based on the responsiveness of local decision makers.

THE STUDENTS

Library media centers face many issues—from lack of funding to censorship. If the political climate is right, the school librarian may want to form a student support group. Sometimes children are the best lobbyists a library can have.

Although aggressively encouraging the students who use the library to lobby their parents or others for additional funding is inappropriate, school librarians need not hide the issue from the students. Explaining funding problems to students is tricky and must be tailored somewhat to their age and ability to understand. Certainly the librarian should not avoid discussing why the library does not have the items the students want when the issue arises, but he or she should be careful not to blame particular individuals for the library's funding problems.

When students are enthusiastic about the library media center and knowledgeable about its needs, they may communicate this enthusiasm and knowledge to their parents. The parents will then become aware that the library requires a certain funding level or other support that it is not receiving in order to provide the services the students want. The parents and even the students may then pressure the appropriate decision makers to increase funding for the school media center.

School media specialists can form student-friends groups as part of their plan to utilize students in a lobbying effort. School clubs are formed around many topics—from business and vocational education to future nurses and athletic clubs. Why not develop a library club at the secondary level? If set up right, the club could eventually help the media center achieve some of its funding goals or help fight censorship if that becomes an issue.

The First Efforts

The library media specialist can no longer rely on the general notion that libraries are good in order to justify an increase in the library's funding base. Communicating the library's needs to decision makers is a major task that can be accomplished in several ways. It can be done indirectly through students who inform their parents about library needs as discussed above. School-library lobbyists can also communicate directly with parents to explain their needs. Although a librarian might believe that the media center's needs are so obvious that any parent with a student at the school would be aware of them, many parents are oblivious to these needs and are unaware of what services a library could provide. Give parents statistics on use, per-pupil library expenditure, statewide average figures, etc. These statistics may make parents recognize that the library has real needs that affect its level of services. Often parents are unaware of a library's potential until they see what an adequately funded school library can provide.

School librarians can also communicate their needs directly to key administrators or decision makers by means of a newsletter, personal letters, personal visits, invitations to participate in library programs, or by any other appropriate means. The direct communication method is advantageous because the librarian can control what is being communicated. In addition, a decision maker or administrator cannot later say that he or she did not notice the library's efforts, good works, or inadequacies. Sometimes library media specialists must "toot their own horn" in order to be noticed.

The Implementation Strategy

SETTING GOALS

As always, the school-library lobbyist needs to determine which goals for the media center might require lobbying efforts. It is important to anticipate problems and to develop a thoughtful and detailed lobbying plan to reach those goals. The library media specialist must then determine who makes the decisions that will affect each of the media center's goals. The target individuals will differ depending on the goal. Different lobbying techniques for each decision maker are necessary depending on each one's relationship to the media center, as described below.

LOBBYING THE TEACHERS

Although teachers will most likely not be primary decision makers on library issues, it is important to get them to use the media center's resources and understand the integral role a good media center can play in a school. Teachers can be extremely effective lobbyists for the school library. If both teachers and the school media specialist ask the administration for additional funding for the school media center, the principal will have a hard time denying such requests outright.

LOBBYING THE PRINCIPAL

A principal as the power decision maker is both good and bad. He or she will be on-site a great deal of the time. On the negative side, even the best media center is not perfect, and the principal will see the library (and librarian!) in full light. If someone has a complaint about the media center or one of its employees, the principal is usually the first to hear about it. The closer someone is to a situation, the more opinionated that person may be. It could be harder to convince the principal that the media center needs more funding if a personality conflict exists between the principal and the librarian. Often the principal makes hiring and firing decisions in regard to the librarian's position. The library media specialist may feel intimidated by the principal's position or relationship and may not lobby as actively as he or she might if the person were removed slightly from the situation.

On the bright side, having daily access to a principal who makes funding decisions can be very beneficial. Knowledge often makes a big difference in a person's ability to be empathetic. The library media specialist is in an ideal situation to educate the principal. If a library complaint deals with poor facilities or lack of materials or technology, the librarian can show the principal the problems and explain them. The principal can quickly verify the deficiencies and respond to the complainant accordingly.

Having easy access to the principal is another great advantage to a principal who is also a decision maker. Although all the teachers may try to garner the principal's attention and time, the library media specialist has an advantage because there is usually only one media center and its role is unique and integral to the mission of school. Some principals rarely leave their offices, but at least the possibility exists to lure an on-site principal to the library media center. If the principal will not go to the center, take the center to the principal! Haul in your entire collection on a certain hot topic; wheel in your first-generation computers; take pictures of the most crowded areas at peak time and present those to the principal. Use the proximity of the principal to your advantage and make sure that he or she knows the media center's problems as well as the services it provides.

The strategy of dealing with a decision maker in your own back yard is as expansive as a librarian's fertile imagination. Create a series of informative or humorous announcements to be read over the school broadcast system. Take the library outside the media center—through booths, book return centers, messages on the back of bathroom doors, etc.—so its presence is obvious throughout the school. The media center needs to appear heavily used and active, so that every time the principal walks by it is full of activity. Again, the fine line between public relations and lobbying is sometimes blurred. However, when the intent is to create an image of the library in the mind of the on-site decision maker, the effort is actually lobbying.

Reinforce whatever your program is by sending an informational memo to the principal explaining your rationale. For example, if you have insufficient funding for acquisitions and decide to cut back on purchase of recreational reading materials, send a message to the principal outlining your plan before you carry it out. If you plan to store materials in classrooms around the school because of lack of space, let the principal know that although you are temporarily dealing with your needs, long-term help is needed. If you are developing a new computer program to help facilitate learning in the library or if you are setting up a monthly series of thematic programming, let the principal know of these ahead of time as well.

LOBBYING THE SUPERINTENDENT OR
OTHER ADMINISTRATOR

If the decision maker is the superintendent or another administrator outside the school, the building-level school-library lobbyist must first make sure that contacting that person is appropriate. You do not want to make your principal look bad or make it appear that you are trying to avoid going through proper channels. If you receive the principal's blessing to lobby actively the next level up, send an initial letter of greeting indicating that you have checked with the principal. Sometimes the principal may react in accordance with the superintendent's wishes, so that even though you have a willing principal the orders are to have the principal remain the official spokesperson for the school's needs.

The district media coordinator may need to lobby the superintendent as his or her first-string target. If so, he or she should use the same techniques outlined throughout this book to inform, educate, and convince the superintendent that the district's media centers' needs are not being met.

Both the building-level librarian and the district media coordinator should place the superintendent on a mailing list for newsletters, announcements of events, and other mailings. In addition, it is usually appropriate to ask the superintendent to speak when the circumstances call for it, such as at a thank-you lunch for media center volunteers, or during National Library Week, National Education Week, National Bicycle Safety Week, National Peanut Week—you get the idea. The library lobbyist may sponsor an open house for all administrators to show them the specific administrative resource materials available to them through the library media center (if you have such a collection) or to demonstrate the latest technology. Try to think of any excuse to bring the individuals to the school media center and then to inundate them with whatever additional messages you want to communicate.

Dealing with superintendents and other administrators at that level may best be left to a parental support group, which can easily contact these individuals with concerns about the library media centers in their children's school. In such a case, the school-library media specialist will need to provide accurate information about the media center's use and needs to the parents. Tips on coordinating volunteers and telephone trees can be found in another part of this book and can be adapted for use with the school media center.

Another group that the school-library lobbyist may want to contact to help lobby the superintendent or other administrator is the local educational association. An educational association will often help lobby the appropriate individuals for increased funding for its members. Although salaries and benefits for school employees are often the primary focus of such a group, it may be willing to advocate for additional funding for the school media program because of its unique role in the school district and the educational system. Avoid calling in this group if traditional conflict or resentment has developed in your district between the administration and the association.

LOBBYING THE SCHOOL BOARD

If the decision maker on a certain issue is the school board, the school media specialist should once again be careful that he or she follows the appropriate channels and receives the appropriate permission. This is not to say that the school-library lobbyist should fear reprisals or feel intimidated in any way. Remember the first amendment! It simply means that in the educational setting, one must be aware of the power hierarchy and follow the district's procedural rules.

As emphasized throughout this chapter, the most effective way to convince a school board about any issue is to solicit the help of supportive parents. They are constituents, while school media specialists are considered individuals with a vested interest, unable to assess objectively the school media center's needs. The school board is not directly responsible to its employees in the same sense that it is responsible to the electorate. The chapters on letter writing, calling, or approaching legislators, etc., will come in handy when working with parent groups.

LOBBYING THE LEGISLATURE

State-school media organizations need to get involved in statewide issues decided by the legislature. Making changes at the state level requires a great deal of forethought and planning. In 1987, only 12–14 states had consistent school-media legislative programs with lobbyists. State school-media organizations need to establish legislative committees and goals now so that eventually they can be an effective legislative force.[10]

Some media specialists may think that few statewide issues concerning school media centers exist. State issues are, however, plentiful. Examples are state categorical aid for school media centers, budget allocations for the state department of education, school media centers as classroom units for funding purposes, money for networking, and many other issues.[11] Many school media specialists feel they do not have the time to deal with problems at the state level. If a problem such as those listed above is at least discussed at a state meeting, a group may find that there are sufficient numbers of interested media specialists to spread the workload. In addition, it is well worth the money at the state level to hire a professional lobbyist to do some of the ongoing lobbying activities that local school media specialists cannot do.[12]

Working together as a state to resolve issues affecting all school media centers can be extremely effective if organized well. Coordinators of one successful state effort suggest a three-year start-up program:

First Year: Appoint a legislative chair who lives in or near the capital and a representative legislative committee with political acumen; provide funds for legislative workshops to develop goals and objectives; and develop a network of politically aware members as key players.

Second Year: Develop a platform of priority concerns; encourage members to visit key legislators; hire a part-time lobbyist; and introduce one bill.

Third Year and Beyond: Develop new platforms annually; and maintain an active membership network.[13]

If little statewide legislative effort for school media centers exists in your state, the above recommendations as well as other recommendations throughout this book will serve to help the school-library lobbyist take the first steps to establish an effective lobbying effort.

THE FOLLOW-UP

As with all lobbying efforts, it is good to reinforce any positive action that a decision maker makes regarding school media centers. Even though such decisions are part of their jobs, principals and superintendents need to be thanked just as often as elected officials.

Doing a postmortem analysis of your efforts and the results is also especially valuable. Try profiling one of the board members in the media center newsletter each month during the year to introduce students and teachers to the school board members. Analyze why your budget was cut after you spent a year attempting to educate the building principal or superintendent about the media center's needs. Was the overall school district budget cut? Did the administrator believe the library was wasting money? Did something else happen that might explain the cut? Perhaps if in-house lobbying did not work it is time to bring in parents and students. Be sensitive to what worked and what didn't and why.

THE LONG-TERM PLAN

As with any long-term plan, the school-library lobbyist must first determine the media center's goals. The librarian must then methodically develop a five-year plan to attain these goals and revise it annually. Carefully planning and orchestrating the lobbying of diverse individuals in the educational setting will pay off, but it is tricky. School librarians must plan around several events peculiar to the education setting. School is in session only nine months of the year in most states. School board members' terms are often staggered in such a way so that there may be a turnover every year. If there is a regular turnover in board members but not much turnover in administration, the administration may influence the board greatly. Both elected and nonelected decision makers affect the library's budget.

A school-library lobbyist may therefore have to plan annual educational strategies and election activities. As a result of the several layers of decision-making, the school library lobbyist will also have to develop several calendars of events and efforts simultaneously to reach the different decision makers. Where possible, the activities should be combined. For example, if you plan an open house, invite not only the principal but also the superintendent and school board members. Even though a principal will usually make the decision affecting the building-level school media center, you may need to lobby the superintendent or the state superintendent of public instruction about an issue at some time.

Lobbying for library media centers is one of the most difficult of all lobbying efforts in the library world because of the power hierarchy and because of the number of individuals who must be lobbied in order to be successful. Plan well, implement wisely, and analyze your successes and failures.

Notes

1. U.S. Dept. of Education, National Center for Education Statistics, Office of Educational Research and Improvement, *Education Statistics; A Pocket Digest, 1990* (1991).

2. Elaine S. Knapp, "A Lesson in School Reform," *State Government News* 33 (September 1990), 9.

3. Alice Ihrig, "Lobbying," in *Funding Alternatives for Libraries*, eds. Patricia Senn Breivik and E. Burr Gibson (Chicago: American Library Association, 1979), 97.

4. *Washakie County School District No. One v. Herschler*, 606 P.2d 310 (Wyo. 1980).

5. Knapp, "A Lesson in School Reform," 9.

6. "Education in Trouble: Kentucky Starts Over," *State Legislatures* 16 (January 1990): 14.

7. Ibid., 14–15.

8. Knapp, "A Lesson in School Reform," 10–11.

9. Ibid., 9.

10. Thomas Hart, "The Legislative Imperative for School Library Media Programs," *Emergency Librarian* 14 (May–June 1987): 19.

11. Ibid., 20, and Mary Margaret Rogers, "Professional Lobbyist and Volunteer Professionals: A Formidable Force for Advocacy," *Emergency Librarian* 14 (May–June 1987): 22–24.

12. Rogers, "Professional Lobbyist and Volunteer Professionals," 22–23.

13. Hart, "The Legislative Imperative for School Library Media Programs," 19.

9

Lobbying for Academic Libraries

Typical Funding Sources

Academic libraries are part of a larger university or college system which can be funded by private, state, and federal sources. Although both private and government-funded systems rely to some degree on tuition and fees for their operating costs, private institutions usually rely more heavily on tuition, while state-funded universities often get a majority of their operating budgets from the state. Both types of institutions seek endowments and foundation gifts for long- and short-term needs and may receive some federal funds (see Chapter 1). A university or college library is usually dependent on its parent institution for the bulk of its ongoing budgetary costs, although many academic library buildings are endowed and named after a benefactor.

When an academic library director wants to lobby for something, he or she faces a power hierarchy similar to that described in Chapter 8 that school libraries face. An academic library director must usually go through several layers of decision makers in order to reach his or her goal.

For example, an academic library director in a state-funded university or college presents the library's budget to its vice-president. That person makes changes and recommendations and presents it to a provost or a president, who makes changes and recommendations before presenting it to a board of trustees or regents. If the college or university is in a higher educational system, then the budget may go to a higher education board or finance committee.

At some point, one of the above groups or individuals submits the budget to the governor. The governor will review it and make recommendations to the legislature. Sometimes, before making recommendations to the legislature, a governor will return the budget to the university and ask for additional cuts. The president and board of trustees must then make additional adjustments in consultation with the academic vice-presidents. A library's budget may therefore return before any final decisions are made.

After the governor makes final budgetary recommendations, a legislative committee will review it and make recommendations to the legislature as a whole. Both houses of the legislature adjust the budget further and make final recommendations which go back to the governor. If the governor has a line-item veto power, he or she may make more changes before approving the final budget. Dozens of variations of the above exist in academic institutions, but the bottom line is that budgeting is extremely difficult for an academic library director in a state-funded university.

In a private institution, the process may be simpler if the budget request filters through fewer individuals or committees. The president or board of trustees of a privately funded college are likely to be the final decision makers. The fewer the number of people to lobby and get to know, the better.

As is the case with school-library lobbyists, each academic library director must determine where the power lies and who makes decisions at each level. The library director can then set a course of action based on the power structure within his or her institution and tailor it to that university library's needs.

Profile of Typical Decision Makers

The individuals who make decisions affecting an academic library will be colleagues or academicians who have over the years obtained administrative positions. As in all cases, some administrators are familiar with library needs, while others rarely used a library even at the graduate level. University administrators are generally overworked and often perceive they have more pressing problems than funding their library.

Administrators with keen insight will understand the unique role the academic library plays in the university or college community. Other administrators will consider the acquisitions budget of a library a large line-item that is easy to cut without hurting any specific academic program. They rationalize further that cutting a percentage of a materials budget does not prohibit all purchases or shut down the library, so it is a prime source of funding with which the university or college budget can be balanced.

At least two levels of administration exist—the president and the academic vice-presidents in charge of different colleges or programs. The lower-level administrators report to the president. They are to some extent influenced by the philosophy of the president. However, in many academic communities individuals are more likely to make independent decisions because tenure lessens the threat of losing a job.

Planning the Lobbying Effort

Directors of academic libraries can follow the advice regarding lobbying internal power hierarchies found in Chapter 8, which deals with schools. They can also generally follow the principles in lobbying legislators and the do's and don'ts outlined in other chapters of this book. They must recognize that differences exist from institution to institution and take into consideration the political realities in their own institutions as they develop their lobbying efforts.

For example, in those institutions where academic library directors do not have a doctorate, they may not be perceived by other academic deans as serious. Academic snobbery still exists. Consequently, directors of academic libraries need to make sure that they measure up to their counterparts in all other ways so that this kind of inadvertent prejudice is forgotten.

Although power hierarchies in universities and colleges exist, it is often university policy to speak through one voice and not approach legislators directly. Academic institutions may even have an administrative legislative liaison to serve in that capacity. Nevertheless, academic institutions probably lend themselves more readily to individual lobbying than their public school counterparts because of tenure, academic freedom, and general freedom from some of the sensitive issues facing public schools.

Lobbying the President

Presidents often come from other institutions, as opposed to being promoted from within the institutions they govern. They are therefore not familiar with the particular library situation at the academic institution when they arrive, and the academic library director must educate them. The president may also have a bias regarding the value of libraries and priority of funding for libraries within the overall institutional needs. The academic library director must determine early in the president's tenure if such a bias exists. If it is a positive bias, the academic library director should take advantage of the situation and present to the president all of the appropriate statistics on library needs and services that had not been funded under a prior administration. If the president's bias is negative, the academic library director needs to use appropriate lobbying techniques to convince the president of the value of an academic library. Although the president may have a personal bias, he or she may also be sensitive to the desires of the board of regents or trustees because he or she is serving at their pleasure.

As in the case of school libraries, appropriate channels should be followed so that a budget request is not held up because of failure to communicate with the appropriate administrator.

Lobbying the Board of Trustees or the Board of Regents

In a state funded institution, the board of regents or trustees is often made up of individuals appointed by the governor, with the advice and consent of the senate. As political appointees, these individuals have a certain allegiance to the philosophy of the governor who appointed them. They may also be sensitive to parents of students, since parents often pay the bill for their children's education. The board may be receptive to lobbying efforts by an associates group or friends group if the library has one organized. Board members may feel discomfort from the political pressures the public might place on them, but their positions are not threatened by unpopular decisions they might make. They are not totally immune from challenge, however. Sometimes a senate will not confirm or reconfirm an appointment, so a threat of being ousted does come into play.

In a private setting, the board may consist of individuals with money and power who are on the board because they want to determine how the college or university is run and because they are major donors. These are not political appointments, and they wield a great deal of power.

The academic library director must become acquainted with a great number of individuals in order to lobby successfully for the library's budget or other bills affecting libraries.

Unique Academic Lobbying Possibilities

This book has repeatedly mentioned the impossible task legislators have of dealing with hundreds of issues. One professor at the University of Southern California suggests that academic institutions can affect state policy by providing comprehensive policy information to legislators.[1] He states that although legislators vote on a lot of bills, each piece of legislation deals with a narrow or specific issue. He suggests that legislators need to understand an issue in a broader context before they can make good decisions on the narrower issue. He concludes that legislators do not understand what happens over time in any given area unless they compare the problem with other states or explore in depth the complexities involved in the problem.[2] As an example, he cited a case in which legislators worked a transportation-financing bill without an overall grasp of how it fit into growth management, into changes in the economy, and into energy questions.[3]

Academic libraries might help legislators have a better overall understanding of issues by providing them with information. Half a dozen research institutions have published books or series of books of public policy issues in their own states just before a legislative session convenes.[4] The editors of these volumes tried to select topics that were "hot." It took so long to write and publish some of the information that some of the issues were moot by the time the books were published. As a result, some editors believe state public policy books are not a good idea.[5] Other editors, such as the one from California, disagree and in fact say that they quit dating their volumes because the books remained timely over the years.[6] Although the university division of public affairs published the volumes, academic library directors may want to help organize or publish a volume for their legislators, since information is their business, and that is what legislators need.

To summarize, academic library directors should first determine whom they need to lobby and then lobby aggressively in order to obtain the budget and sponsorship they desire. As always, academic library directors must remain sensitive to the internal power structure of their own institutions. The academic library director can and perhaps should play a vital role in the informational needs of state legislators or the board of regents or trustees.

Notes

1. Pate Wunnicke, "Advice from Academe," *State Legislatures* 17 (March 1991): 26.
2. Ibid.
3. Ibid.
4. Ibid.
5. Ibid.
6. Ibid., 27.

10

Strategy of the State Library's Lobbying the State Legislature

A state library that wants to pass legislation must lobby differently from public libraries because it is an arm of the state. Depending on the internal organization of the state government, it may or may not be an independent agency. In Wyoming, the state library was independent until reorganization made it part of the Department of Administration. As an independent unit, it presented its budget directly to members of the Appropriations Committee and answered to them as an agency. As part of a department, it makes its proposal to the head of the department, who makes priorities among all its agencies and then presents budget requests to the Appropriations Committee. When a state library stands alone, it may have more power to be persuasive because it is not one of several agencies represented by a nonlibrarian who may or may not be able to give the legislature the best information about the state library's needs and who may or may not be supportive of libraries in general.

In addition, some states do not allow their own agencies to lobby the legislature. The state library must rely on public libraries or others to do their lobbying for budgetary and other legislative needs. State librarians need to be sensitive to their own political role and know how it fits within its state structure.

It is sad to say that many legislators see state employees as inefficient, uncaring, and lazy bureaucrats.[1] Dealing with legislatures is tricky, but when legislators consider you one of "their employees," it becomes especially difficult. The role of the state librarian is very political and takes a lot of political acumen. State libraries should therefore strive to be as useful to legislators as possible. State library personnel must make state library services to their legislature available, useful, and visible. It is important not to play favorites among legislators, such as by giving members of the budget committee a state library card but not offering the same amenity to other legislators, even if one committee has more say in your budget than another. It is also important to have a written policy regarding legislative interactions so that decisions are uniform.

Develop an aggressive service program for legislators and inform them on a regular basis what it is that the state library does that no other libraries do. Certainly, the state legislature is one of the state library's major constituents. If legislators and legislative aides are not using the state library's resources for research, then the state library should offer a training program or informational brochure on what is available to legislators. Many legislatures sponsor legislative schools to inform new legislators about the legislative process, to show them around, and to educate them about some of the more complex legislative issues. State librarians should try to get on the agenda and give all new legislators a library card, a tour of the facility, and an informational presentation. The state library should let legislators know that staff is available for research and reference services. Legislators will be impressed with good, friendly help from a government agency. It is hard for a legislator to understand what state agencies actually do, and the more familiar they are with the state library's services, the better off the state library will be.

Note

1. I believe that most state employees are hard-working individuals who care about doing a good job for the state.

11

The Long-Term Plan

Libraries at all levels should develop a long-term plan for lobbying at the state level, even if they are not particularly politically active and the plan is minimal. The first question asked is usually, "Where do I start?" An easy place to begin is with the elections of decision makers.

Election Activities

A librarian must include election dates and activities in any long-term plan. To wait until someone is elected is to lose a tremendous opportunity to influence an elected official. Planning election activities is an easy place to start making a long-term plan. Primaries take place at a variety of times throughout the United States, but general elections occur in November. Librarians need to determine which dates are critical within their own states, get out their calendars, and start plotting some election activities.

It is important for the local librarian to determine which candidates will be most supportive of libraries if they are elected. Library supporters can use an incumbent's record to make this judgment, but they have to determine a newcomer's position. This can be done in a number of ways. The most common techniques are candidate issue questionnaires, candidate forums, or individual meetings with special interest groups or subcommittees.

Candidate Issue Questionnaires

Every candidate, regardless of whether that person is running at the local, state, or federal level, receives a great number of issue questionnaires from special interest groups. The candidate often, but not always, completes and returns the questionnaires. The special interest groups use the information to encourage their members to vote for or against certain candidates.

Sometimes the questionnaires are straightforward, and sometimes they are loaded. For example, one group may send a questionnaire with a page of information about the question before they ask the question. The information does not state the organization's position on the question (although often a person can guess it by reading or knowing about the group), and the organization's purpose is to educate the candidate as well as to determine the candidate's position. Providing some background information is probably a good tactic. Candidates are under pressure, and if the questionnaire at least gives them a little background, they appreciate it.

Some special interest groups provide a paragraph or more about the issues but do so in a way that also reveals their strong bias. Whether or not it is intentional, the purpose may not be to educate the candidates but to warn them that this is the position of a great number of individuals and if they answer the questionnaire wrong they are likely to lose a great number of votes.

Finally, some questionnaires consist of questions based on the assumption that the candidates will know the pros and cons of an issue. Questionnaires of this sort put the candidate in the position of either researching the issues if he or she is unfamiliar with them or of calling the group that puts out the questionnaire. Either option takes more work at a time when the candidate may be especially busy. Librarians at all levels should develop a questionnaire for candidates. As previously mentioned, probably the most effective is an informational questionnaire without the inferences of strong bias. Every candidate may become an elected official, and it is important to start off on the right foot. If the questionnaire provides background information, however brief, the candidate appreciates it. That person can still qualify the answer by stating that he or she needs additional information to make an informed decision. On the other hand, the candidate can also state that he or she supports the legislation or issue based on the information supplied. Elected officials listen most closely and learn most effectively right before they are elected! Librarians should take advantage of this vulnerability and educate the candidates as much as possible.

Candidate Forums

A second type of interaction with candidates that librarians should build into their long-term plan is candidate forums. Many, many groups ask candidates to speak to them before an election and either answer questions from the audience or give a presentation on whatever special interest is involved. Many groups do a poor job in this area because they don't understand how many issues an elected official must face and how busy candidates are. When librarians organize a candidate's forum, their first purpose should be to educate the candidates about library problems. Most candidates believe they understand libraries and library problems because, "What can be complicated about a library?" One county commissioner told me that he couldn't figure out why a public library needed more than one employee to point the patrons in the right direction of the books they wanted! He quickly added, however, that perhaps a second person was necessary to tell stories to the "kiddies." A candidate who wants to win and please the electorate during a campaign is receptive to hearing the library's problems.

If librarians decide to sponsor a candidate forum, they should ask the candidate to participate as far in advance as possible and send appropriate background information to each candidate prior to the meeting. The information should include everything the librarian would want that candidate to know if he or she were an elected official. The serious candidates will read and absorb that information. The librarian-lobbyist should also send to the participating candidates a format explanation. It is good to let them know what to expect before they arrive.

The forum should then reinforce the information the candidate received by making sure the candidate hears the library's problems again. Start the forum by having the head librarian or lobbyist summarize the high points of the information the candidates received. Different library employees could also give statements about their department's problems if they are pertinent. Other library employ-ees could summarize particular problems facing them if there is a legislative or political solution. The idea is to ensure that the candidates are educated about the library before they have to give their opinion about it. This type of format serves not only to educate the candidates and future legislators but also to make them feel comfortable about their own answers. Candidates will remember which group grilled them unfairly, especially if they were embarrassed.

After the library gives its presentation, each candidate should be invited to share his or her views on what they have just heard. The format should include time at the end for questions, answers, interaction, and informal discussion if possible. It is important to allow candidates a little time to speak to what they believe is important. If they received the appropriate information prior to the meeting, they will be ready with their own thoughts and viewpoints about the situation.

Candidate Interviews

Some groups request time with each candidate for an individual interview by a legislative subcommittee. As at a job interview, a candidate is asked a series of questions and discusses issues with this small group, which then makes its recommendations of support to the larger group. If a library or library association decides to go this route, it should follow all the recommendations noted above for a candidate's forum. The idea is to educate the candidates while also determining their position on library issues. If a group goes straight for a candidate's position on an issue without educating that person, it loses a tremendous opportunity, even if that person is not subsequently elected.

Summary

Dealing with the information gained from questionnaires, candidate forums, and interviews can be very tricky. Backing the "wrong horse" is detrimental. Yet, a librarian may pay for a long time if he or she ignores an unsupportive candidate and that person wins. The best idea is to provide the public and members of the library association or whoever sponsors the questionnaire, forum, or interview with the answers to the questions given by each candidate. Often the answers speak for themselves, and the voters do not need a special interest group (if you can call libraries that) to place a value on what the candidates say. In fact, some members of the public resent being told how to vote or being given a judgmental analysis of an answer that they can read themselves. On the other hand, if one candidate clearly supports library issues and another does not, the library may want to endorse publicly the supportive candidate and state why. Librarians will have to judge their own communities to decide what to do with the information gathered in this way.

Postelection, Presession Activities

Once elections are over, a different type of lobbying begins. It is more competitive in that prior to election, candidate hopefuls wanted to please the librarians. Now that the elections are over, often legislators are less likely to listen and more likely to opine. In any case, librarians need to plan the next general series of events when organizing a long-term timetable. The day-by-day watchdogging and lobbying of bills described earlier in this book is not something that can be scheduled too far in advance. Librarians need to determine legislative meeting dates, legislative library day, and any other annual events that the legislators and librarians can plan ahead of time.

An easy event to put on the calendar is the date of the legislative session. State legislatures meet anywhere from once every two years (Kentucky) to year-round (Massachusetts, Michigan) to two sessions per year (New York, Illinois). (See Table 4, page 79.) However, most legislatures begin their annual meetings in January. As discussed earlier, the months of November and December become important months to make sure that the legislators know and understand any potential library legislation planned. If librarians pick a date during this period for a presession meeting with legislators and make it an annual affair, it is more effective than a last-minute, "Hey, the legislature is going to start soon. We'd better get in touch with our representatives soon."

Scheduling an annual legislative event on the long-term calendar is an excellent plan. If legislators know about it early and know that it is an annual event, they will anticipate it and plan for it themselves. Any kind of event will do. Keep in mind that what makes it effective is its annual and predictable nature. At the event, whether it is a tea, a lunch, a meeting at the library, a going-away party, a Christmas party, or a legislative review party, the librarians need to communicate their legislative agenda to the legislators.

If the librarians have no specific legislative agenda during a particular year, they should still sponsor the event and turn it into a legislator-appreciation event. If the legislators know that every November or December before the session the banks, the railroads, the oil companies, the insurance companies, *and* the libraries all sponsor get-togethers, libraries will begin to stick in their minds as a group to which they must be sensitive politically.

Librarians also need to include on their long-term calendar a date during this presession time after the annual event to send the legislators a note or card reminding them of the librarians' legislative agenda for the year and thanking them for their support. Even if the librarians believe they accomplished this task at the annual event, a note of thanks for the legislator's upcoming support of the library agenda is still appropriate. The note should contain the name and phone numbers of the library contact person in case legislators have any questions during the session that need answers in a hurry. A librarian can pick any date after the annual event but before the session for this particular interaction.

Librarians need to be aware of the timing in each state for submitting draft bills to the legislative drafting office, for introduction of bills, for hearing a bill in committee, for closing the general file, and for any other important step in the legislative process. These dates should be noted on the calendar accordingly. This information is available from the legislators themselves or, in some states, through a legislative service office dealing with questions such as this.

Postsession Activities

The only time period left of each year is the postsession, which could last from a month to over a year and a half, depending on the state. Librarians in states with full-time legislatures have to plan a lot more activities during the session. In those states, legislators often schedule a certain number of days to return to their districts for citizen input. It is important for librarians to know when those days are and schedule a meeting, if possible. The legislator's staff will know this information and should be able to schedule meetings periodically if necessary. In those states with part-time legislatures or where the legislature is full-time but meets only for six months or so, librarians should also note these dates on their long-term calendars and plan to contact their legislators in a variety of ways already discussed.

Many groups plan postsession meetings and invite legislators to tell their members what the legislature accomplished in the group's area of interest. Librarians need to plan an annual postsession luncheon or meeting at which legislators can speak about or be on a panel to discuss library legislation. Such a meeting accomplishes two goals. First, it makes the legislators accountable to librarians and gives them a chance to follow up on what they told the librarians prior to the session. Second, if the legislator was involved in as many different issues as most legislators are, it will require the legislator to review what the legislature did "to" or "for" libraries. This review again reinforces in a legislator's mind that librarians are a group to reckon with and that library legislation is important. A postsession meeting also gives librarians a chance to reward and thank the legislators for their efforts. If it is an annual event, similar to the chamber of commerce lunches at which legislators describe business legislation, it becomes more significant, and legislators know that a large library support group exists.

Librarians may want to note on their calendars the meeting dates of legislative committees that might sponsor legislation affecting libraries. This kind of scheduling may be more appropriate for the statewide library lobbyist than for the local librarian. The committee work between sessions is often very important, but it is costly for local librarians to travel a long way simply to listen to a committee for potential mention of library problems. The association-library lobbyist will attend if necessary and try to determine ahead of time whether or not librarians need to be present to testify.

If committee meetings are held in different parts of the state, librarians should attend the meetings in their areas and introduce themselves to the legislators involved with library legislation. The legislators will know that librarians are involved and interested, and the meeting will also give a librarian an excuse to write a letter to a legislator from another district if that legislator is key to a particular piece of legislation. For example, "Dear Senator Ely: It was a pleasure meeting you last fall when you attended the committee meeting in Shelby. I understand that you are on the committee that reviews legislation dealing with library aid . . . " Decision makers are more likely to read your communication carefully and answer it if they met and interacted with you previously, even though you are not a primary constituent.

On this long-term lobbying calendar, the librarian should also note when National Library Week is and any other activities the library itself is planning. The librarian should send invitations or, at the minimum, annual reports to the legislators in the library's district about all the activities taking place at the library during the year. If the library or the friends have a newsletter, all legislators should receive copies. If a legislator receives information on a continuing basis from the librarian on the vast number of activities and use the library receives, the legislator is going to be more impressed than if the only interaction is an annual legislative dinner. Most legislators are less aware of what goes on at a library than are local decision makers.

On the local level, the librarians should follow all of the above suggestions for election activities because the same procedure holds true for both local and state elections, although local decision makers will most likely meet year-round on a daily, weekly, or monthly basis. Librarians should note when the local decision makers meet and plan to send a library representative whenever possible. All other activities recommended above in terms of ongoing communication with decision makers should also be followed.

Library legislation or budget requests may not occur every year, but when they do, librarians want to have laid the groundwork already for its successful passage. Having a long-term calendar with important events and reminders and acting on it faithfully will help immensely in preparing for the day when action is necessary.

*   *   *   *   *

It is not too late for the library director, the library staff, trustees, school administrators, university presidents, friends, and supporters of all kinds to begin planning a well-orchestrated lobbying effort. Many of these individuals are lobbying in some fashion already. A coordinated, thoughtful campaign will increase the likelihood of a successful effort.

Librarians need to let decision makers know that libraries exist, are flourishing, and, with the help of the decision makers, will continue to be dynamic and responsive symbols of our great nation.

Index

Academic libraries
   federal funding legislation
      and, 5, 7–9
   lobbying for, 168–73
   and state funding, 60, 168–69
Access, to information, 13–15
Accuracy, of information, 96, 112
Ad valorem taxes, 125
Amendments, to legislation 71–72,
   76–77, 87, 106–7, 110
American Booksellers Association,
   15
American Library Association
   (ALA), 4, 8, 10–11
Appropriation (funding), 3–4
Attorney general, 89–90
Authorization (funding), 3–4
Awards, 92–93

Bills. *See* Legislation
Boards of trustees. *See* Library
   boards; Regents

Brochures, 37
Budget lobbying techniques
   for academic libraries, 168–73
   for public libraries, 132–35
   for school libraries, 156–66
Budget preparation/presentation
   for academic libraries, 169–70
   for public libraries, 129–35
   for school libraries, 155
Bureaucrats. *See* Decision makers

Calendaring process, 75–76
Calling trees, 39–40
Campaign contributions, 115
Campaigns, coordinated, 78–93
Censorship, 13–15
Child Protection and Obscenity
   Enforcement Act of 1988, 15
Citizen-lobbyists, 24–25
College administrators, and fund-
   ing, 169–70
Committee hearings, 71, 73, 109–11

185

Lisa Kinney is a librarian and a lawyer, and now a legislator. She was director of a county library in Wyoming for seven years and has served as a Wyoming state senator since 1984. A sole practitioner of law since 1987, she owns a law bar review course and is currently documentation officer for the University of Wyoming American Heritage Center. The mother of three, she spends her time juggling professional and parental duties.